DECLARE

The Secret to Submerging into God's Presence

Prayer Series Book 1

Terry Scott Bonner

Endorsements

"The body of Christ is moving into new realms of His presence and continues to usher in the present revival that is transforming nations. We are seeing a generation that has given itself to prayer. If you are looking for a simple yet insightful guide to prayer, Pastor Terry has done this with *Declare*. I appreciate the personal touch that he brings with his own journey in prayer. He generously gives keys that lay a foundation to bring understanding to a lifestyle of prayer."

—Eric Johnson
Lead Pastor, Bethel Church in Redding, California

"May this book serve as a spiritual defibrillator to shock the heart of the body of Christ back into her high calling of effective prayer and accurate intercession."

—Steve Carpenter
Highway 19 Ministries in Jerusalem, Israel

"This is not only a timely book on prayer, it is a strategic war manual that challenges you to fervently pursue God, provides practical strategy and understanding of how to pray, and gives hope for personal and corporate restoration. A must read!"

—JoAnne Meckstroth
US Director, Northwest Region
Regional Coordinator, AGLOW International

"Prayer is not a decoration that we wear, but a declaration of dependence we declare! Many people talk about prayer, and a few others live a lifestyle of prayer. Terry is such a man who has not only himself been inspired to pray but is leading a congregation in a lifestyle of prayer. His church is a place where the atmosphere has been altered by a leadership that has a continued desire to meet with God, which has infected the entire congregation. I have to warn you that the following pages of this book will be harmful to your flesh while inspiring your spirit. You have to ask yourself the question, do I desire God to change my life? True men and women of God desire change long before they ever have to. This book will challenge you to permanently transform your lifestyle to become a prayer warrior. So as you read through this spiritual workout book, keep your head up and your knees down! God will do the rest."

—Jayme Montera
President of Mercy Seat Ministries Midwest and Awakening a Generation

sub'merge (Dictionary.com)

1. to be enveloped.

2. to cover or overflow; immerse.

3. to be covered or lost from sight.

4. to be hidden from view.

Scripture quotations taken from the Amplified® Bible,
Copyright © 1954, 1958, 1962, 1964, 1965, 1987 by The Lockman Foundation
Used by permission. (www.Lockman.org)

Scripture taken from the NEW AMERICAN STANDARD BIBLE®, Copyright © 1960, 1962, 1963, 1968, 1971, 1972, 1973, 1975, 1977, 1995 by The Lockman Foundation. Used by permission.

THE HOLY BIBLE, NEW INTERNATIONAL VERSION®, NIV® Copyright © 1973, 1978, 1984, 2011 by Biblica, Inc.™ Used by permission. All rights reserved worldwide.

Scripture taken from the New King James Version®. Copyright © 1982 by Thomas Nelson, Inc. Used by permission. All rights reserved.

Scripture quotations marked (NLT) are taken from the Holy Bible, New Living Translation, copyright © 1996, 2004, 2007 by Tyndale House Foundation. Used by permission of Tyndale House Publishers, Inc., Carol Stream, IL 60188. All rights reserved.

Scripture quotations marked "MSG" or "The Message" are taken from The Message. Copyright 1993, 1994, 1995, 1996, 2000, 2001, 2002. Used by permission of NavPress Publishing Group.

First Printing: 2007 Good Catch Publishing
ISBN-13: 978-1534686991
ISBN-10: 1534686991

For further information contact Terry Scott Bonner at 1.425.220.1713
terrybonnerbooks@gmail.com
Printed in the United States of America

Acknowledgements

To my wife Jenni and my children Shaylie and Trey who were always a great support and encouragement as I wrote this book. I wrote this book for you and our future generations. It will serve as a reminder of the legacy of prayer in our family.

A special thank you to my editor, Dori Harrell. Your feedback was always helpful and professional. Your encouragement to me was priceless.

Thank you, Lynnette Bonner, for the design cover and mentoring me through the process of publishing.

Thank you, Jon Stewart, for the inside design of the book.

Special thanks to the staff, friends, and family of Jakes House Church and Destiny International School of Ministry. It has been a fun journey. Thank you for the privilege of being the Director of the Prayer School.

To John Knoch, Jeshu Ram, Keith Kippen, George Keller, James Wilson, Toby Mitchell, Joe Clapper and others who have walked this journey of prayer with me.

Finally, to the Prayer School that I have the honor of directing. We live this book every Thursday night.

I dedicate this book to the living memory of Edward McKendree Bounds.

> E. M. Bounds books are unfailing wells for a lifetime of spiritual water-drawing. They are hidden treasures, wrought in the darkness of dawn and the heat of the noon, on the anvil of experience, and beaten into wondrous form by the mighty stroke of the divine. They are living voices whereby he, being dead, yet speak!
>
> —Claude Chifton

Your books have inspired me to greater levels of prayer.

Contents

INTRODUCTION

This is a clarion call to abandon the weak and ineffective use of ritualistic prayer and embrace the biblical method of hiding under the shadow of God—in other words...**submerging into the presence of God through prayer.**

> Stars slowly cascading across the evening sky,
> windblown invisible
> across the barren landscape of our lives.
> Water...cold, fluid, and refreshing,
> the ocean, ever leaving and returning in cadence
> with the pull of the evening moon.
> The rhythm of life and nature combine
> to create within me a heart desire
> for peace, contentment, and serenity.

I wrote this poem during a moment of prayer and contemplation on a beach in Mexico. It is amazing how prayer can unlock a deeper way of appreciating God's movement in nature. This book is for the vast majority of people who have struggled to establish a consistent prayer life over the years.

No More Camping Out Spiritually

A friend of mine was spraying room freshener in his church sanctuary. His wife walked in and asked, "Why are you spraying that in here?" He replied, "I am sick of the smell of death in our church!" Does your church or family have the smell of death or the smell of life? What do people feel and experience when they walk into your church for the first time? Many people have said to me, "Pastor, I can feel that something is different here. I feel the freedom and the prayers that are prayed in this place." Our first-time visitors are affected by the spiritual atmosphere in the room. They may be impressed by the bulletin and assisted by the ushers, but they are changed by what they experience. The welcome team and the perfectly executed service plan are not going to create the spiritual atmosphere people are looking for. They are not transformed by the ability to design beautiful buildings and entertain the masses. I want them to experience the true atmosphere-changing power of God.

This book will shake up your complacency and enable your inner person to soar to new heights. It is designed to uproot the tent pegs of your spiritual capacity and cause you to move forward with the cloud of God's presence. Camping out, or settling in spiritually, is destructive to your spiritual life. You need to develop a lifestyle of expectancy in prayer to counter this fatal disease. Here are some results of not moving forward spiritually:

- We tend to fight each other when we are not fighting the enemy (infighting).
- We get too comfortable in our surroundings and are unwilling to move.
- We get nervous when God begins to do something out of our comfort zones.

Are you satisfied in His presence? If so, check your spiritual campground and make sure your tent pegs aren't dug too deeply. The definition of the word expectation is "a reasonable belief that something will happen." Your prayer life must be marked by a tremendous level of expectancy. Most people do not believe God can and will do something amazing in their lives. They believe God might show up someday, if they are lucky. Luck has nothing to do with it. God always moves according to His covenant promises (this will be discussed later in the book). I believe that expectation is more of preparation meeting opportunity. As believers, we do not believe in chance. We believe is destiny. God's desire to impact your life is often stymied by your lack of spiritual preparation. We need to prepare our lives so we are ready. What would you do if God asked you to go to Africa today? Could you do it? Would you do it? One time God said to me, "I won't send you to Africa." I was hurt by that statement because I had always prided myself on being willing to go anywhere God asked. He said, "You don't even have a passport! You wouldn't make it through the airport." That made sense. Now, every person in our family has a passport, and we have emergency money set aside. Just in case.

Start Your Spiritual Journey Today

"The American Way" is a pioneering mantra and philosophy that teaches people to carve out their own pathways through the forest of life. Many consider it a badge of honor to say that they are in need of no one. This self-made-man concept couldn't be further from the truth. The kingdom life is a way of living that teaches us to embrace our relationships with God and others. We are not islands unto ourselves. We must learn to completely trust the faithfulness of God and find strength in the people we have built healthy relationships with. It is only under the shadow of His wings that we can truly find safety, rest, fulfillment, and destiny. This book will lead you on a great journey. You will embark on a spiritual voyage that will carry you quickly away from the selfishness of this world and the religion of the church, and into a dynamic and exciting relationship with God.

Losing Touch with God

When used properly, this book will increase the power and effectiveness of your personal prayer life. Our community prayer will be even more powerful when we increase the number of people who are praying daily in the secret places.

Have you ever heard of the Tent of Meeting? God commanded Moses to create a special tent, located outside the camp, away from the everyday business of life. Moses was directed to go there daily and meet with God. God intended separation in order to clean up our communications. His desire was for us to have communication that was free from the pollution of fear and worry that we so easily operate in.

The following excerpt is my personal opinion and may or may not be historically correct. The command by God to create the Tent of Meeting came on the heels of the golden-calf incident. Remember, Moses had gone up the mountain (represents the presence of God) to communicate with God. The people were in a rush and became very nervous. They wanted a quick word from the Lord and a fast-track solution to their problem. In rebellion, they tried to force God into answering their request by creating and worshipping a golden calf. They literally replaced the idea of praying and waiting on God with a man-made religious act they hoped would connect them with Him. The church of today is steeped in a formula of conducting religious exercises rather than practicing the time-honored method of praying.

Desiring a Fast-Track Solution to Your Problem Only Hinders Your Spiritual Development

Isn't it funny that we always describe the failure of others as rebellion, ye we describe our acts of disobedience as "incidents" or "situations." Well, the golden-calf situation and the reactions by God and Moses, which resulted in many deaths, created such a sense of fear in the people that they allowed this fear to cripple their communication with God. Remember, they would say things like, "Moses, we want you to hear from God for us. We don't want to hear God's voice for ourselves because it frightens us." I believe God intended for the whole camp of Israel to gather at the Tent of Meeting to hear from the Lord, not just Moses. Yet the Bible says that when Moses went into the Tent of Meeting, the people stayed at the openings of their own tents. They were afraid to come near the presence of God and hear His voice. God's desire was daily contact with His people. Yet fear and worry condemned them to secondhand communication. God's desire for us is daily contact, yet fear and worry condemns us to secondhand communication as well.

This guide was created for you to use on a daily basis in your own personal secret place of prayer. My desire is that you would not stand at the door of your tent but that you would enter the Tent of Meeting and begin to hear the voice of the Lord for yourself. Group prayer meetings are great but are not a substitute for your secret meetings with the King.

Desperate for Intimacy with God

We are social creatures by nature. For instance, we will deprive ourselves of precious sleep by staying up late at night to talk with friends on the phone. Why? Studies have shown that living without communication causes a person to lose his or her sanity or the will to live. Communication is a basic emotional need that we all require. God-communication is an even more vital component to our emotional and spiritual development.

Inmates will risk torture or harsh punishment by breaking the rules and sending secret messages to fellow prisoners just to communicate. Why? Because we all need communication. Our hearts yearn for it, we love it, and we can't live without it. Powerful prayer starts with a desperation for more intimacy and communication with God.

King David spent more than ten years running for his life in the desert. His mentor and leader wanted to kill him and discredit everything he had done. Yet in the midst of this chaos and pressure, David could say, "O God, You are my God; with deepest longing I will seek You; My soul (my life my very self) thirst for you, my flesh longs and sighs for You, in a dry and weary land where there is no water" (Psalm 63:1 AMP).

We must be desperate enough to realize that without communication with God we are dead. Our motto in life should be

Psalm 28:1 MSG: "Don't turn a deaf ear when I call you, GOD. If all I get from you is deafening silence, I'd be better off in the Black Hole." Prayer is not preparation for ministry—prayer is ministry, and it is our breath of life!

True Leaders of Intercession

There have been many books written about the modern-day generals or leaders of intercession. One such book named several men and women who were used by God to do amazing things. My problem with that book stems from the fact that many of the leaders mentioned later fell into moral failure, depression, or insanity. They started well but couldn't finish strong.

I believe the true generals of intercession were left out of that book, men like E. M. Bounds, A. W. Tozer, Leonard Ravenhill, and Paul Yongii Cho. I want to learn about men and women who have made a long-term impact in this world for prayer. An impact that lasts more than ten or twenty years. I want to know about prayer warriors whose words and teachings impact and challenge the church long after they have departed this earthly realm.

Wasting Time in Prayer?

Prayer is not a waste of time. Rather, it is a process of redeeming time. To *redeem* means to buy back, repair, restore, or to make good. We can restore everything that has been stolen from us by the enemy. As you know, we all have broken or lost areas of our lives that we need God to fix or repair. Even our ideas and desires need to be redeemed. Some of our greatest ideas sound good but are only made great through dedicated prayer. At times, we fail to understand the most foundational biblical truth: we can hear the direction of God for our lives through prayer.

> *You must expand your prayer grid in order to*
> *experience more of God.*
> —Ryan Wyatt

Few Agonizers

Many organizers, few agonizers
Many players and payers, few prayers
Many singers, few clingers
Many pastors, few wrestlers
Many fears, few tears
Much fashion, little passion
Many interferers, few intercessors
Many writers, but few fighters
—Leonard Ravenhill

CHAPTER 1
BECOME A SPIRITUAL REVOLUTIONARY

A desire for God that cannot break the chains of sleep is a weak thing indeed.

—E. M. Bounds

A Warrior's Tale

Soldiers weren't meant to just watch the fight. There is something inherent in every warrior. It is the desire for battle.

I remember arriving in Catania, Sicily, where I was stationed as a military policeman. Terrorists had just detonated a bomb at the USO in Rome that week, and our naval base was on high alert. We were told that another bombing was imminent and that our base was on a list of targeted facilities. Every day we stood guard, waiting for the attack that would never come. Each night we checked passenger buses for bombs and patrolled the housing complex to protect sleeping family members. Kevlar helmets, flak jackets, M-16 rifles, and .45 caliber pistols were our best friends and closest allies. For several weeks, we were on alert and were confident we would find ourselves in the middle of a violent terrorist attack. Gratefully, that attack never came, but it brings up another issue.

The next two years of my life were spent patrolling the base, arresting drunks, and training for possible terrorist situations. There is something inside an eighteen-year-old kid that longs for a battle, and something strange about training to fight but never going to battle.

For too long, the church has been satisfied with merely talking about a spiritual war yet standing at a safe distance with our well-groomed services and our self-protecting grace theology. But talk becomes cheap when we consistently remain at a safe distance from the spiritual confrontation so as to never get hurt or offended. Our battle is not against flesh and blood but against principalities, powers, rulers of this dark age, and spiritual hosts in high places (different levels of the demonic realm). This being the case, we must realize that Sunday church lunches, feeding programs, Easter productions, and daycare centers, while valid, are not the way we were intended to fight. Those ministries are for service and relationship building, which are critical to the overall health of churches. But they are not our key method of warfare. Special Forces soldiers are not given the Medal of Honor for training. They are awarded medals based of heroism and valor in actual battle. We fight a spiritual battle with spiritual weapons—namely prayer. Prayer is our contact point to the spirit realm, and it is our *chief* weapon to use against the enemy.

Churches in America have been great at talking about prayer, but we have not been good at practicing it. We even sing great worship songs about the necessity of prayer. Yet most of our churches are void of any real prayer power. We justify this by saying we are too busy or that we already have intercession teams that pray for us. Every church has a group of ladies that meets secretly in the designated prayer room. Are we relying on these dear women to be our prayer covering? If so, we are dead, and our churches will be graveyards. Prayer was never intended to be a side ministry of the local church. It was designed to be the culture and primary vehicle of interaction between God and man for the whole church. The Bible says, "My house shall be a house of prayer for all nations." *My house* referring to the church and to your family and to you as an individual. Prayer must be restored to its rightful place as the culture-setting, attitude-changing, mind-renewing vehicle of hope.

Frustration sets in when we realize our lives are not reflecting the supernatural elements of the kingdom. You may feel unsettled and eager to do something...anything. This spiritual anxiety will lead to you push your agenda and your timetable for what you consider your ministry or destiny. If this frustration is not dealt with and if the drive for success in ministry and life is not protected with patience, you will develop the dangerous tendency to rush into life and make vital decisions based on a self-preserving philosophy of "If I don't do this now, life will pass me by."

Patience-based discipleship enables us to be in life for the long haul. We begin to understand that destiny is not a place. Rather, it is the journey. Therefore, my success in life is not dependent on how large my ministry is or how much money I make. It is dependent on becoming like Christ, and that takes a lifetime. Frustration is our way of dealing with the disease called "I want it now." But that begs a question. What do you want now? Do you want success as defined by the world around you, or do you want to be a man or woman who is filled with grace, faith, and love? Do you want to be controlled and driven by your volcanic emotions, or would you rather calmly walk out your destiny in peace? It is up to you. God has given you the ability to decide your path in life. You can choose your own path and speed up the timetable of your destiny. Or you can choose the path and natural rhythm of discipleship that God has created for you. And that is easily found through the daily habits of prayer and Bible meditation. Spiritual growth should never be rushed, though it should be pursued.

A friend of mine once preached, "You can't always do your own thing. You have to be told." What he meant was we need a command from God tattooed on our hearts that says, "This is why you are on the planet. This is what I want you to do." Frustration is limited when we begin to operate our lives and ministries based on a true word from God rather than a desperate desire for success and notoriety. Praying is the system we use to receive the word from God.

God's people are preparing for battle, and a battle cry is rising from deep within their very souls. Their spirits are stirred and long to fight for their families, jobs, and relationships. The vast army of God, *which is the local church*, must be mobilized and organized to fight, and soldiers must be led into the great battle. I am a firm believer in having a personalized, strategic plan for prayer. Jesus got up early morning while it was still dark and while people were sleeping. He arose with purpose. The purpose to pray and connect with God. He climbed a mountain every morning to pray. That is a dedication to the idea of prayer. See Matthew 14:23, John 6:3, and Matthew 5:1

Sunday morning church is not the battlefield. It is only a time of preparation and training for the real battle. Strategic instruction and life-changing declarations on Sunday morning enable us to fight properly in prayer the rest of the week. Spiritual confrontation is during prayer, when captives are released and ground is taken back. We must take excited, grounded, and prepared warriors and march them boldly to the front lines of spiritual battle. Jesus proved this theory. He prayed in the morning and then walked out His daily life in victory.

Warriors Are Supposed to Die
So why are we spending so much time trying to live? The Bible teaches us to die daily to self, yet we love to live. Living for today and living for yourself seems to be the motto of the modern-day church. Long gone are the days of seeking the Lord and praying until something changes. I declare that God is calling us to a fresh mantle of dying to self and extreme living for God.

Soldiers who know they are going to die anyway make the best fighters. If you have nothing to lose, then fight on. If you are lost to the world and found in Christ, then you will be prepared to fight without reservation and without fear. When we finally get a revelation that we are dead anyway, then we will rise up and begin to wage war like real heroes of the faith.

When I Die, Let It Be Said...
When I die, let it be said of me that I was a man of prayer. When

all is said and done and my time on earth is over, I intend to be another cog in the machine of prayer that has been impacting this planet for thousands of years.

My greatest heroes are not sports stars, movie actors, or billionaires, although the person who created coffee is definitely high on my list. Those who have impacted my life the most were the fathers of the prayer movement. These were men who gave their lives to the task of teaching a generation to pray. Men like Andrew Murray, Leonard Ravenhill, E. M. Bounds, A. W. Tozer, David Brainerd, Praying John Hyde, and many others. These men taught me to take the sacred act of prayer and save it from drowning in the murky waters of religion.

An ancient path of prayer exists that has been followed for thousands of years. Some men and women have selflessly kept the machine of prayer operating day after day, giving no thought to the future. These prayer warriors did not know that they were building a legacy for others to follow. **Daniel** taught us the discipline of set prayer times and freed us from our grossly mistaken belief that anything disciplined is religious. He prayed three times a day, every day, and would not alter that ritual even if it cost him his life. It was said that his prayers were answered immediately by God. **Elijah** prayed, and the rains stopped for three years. **Elisha** prayed, and his servant's eyes were open to the spirit realm, and he saw an angelic army. **Moses** prayed and changed the mind of God. In the book of Acts, the believers prayed, and the place where they prayed was shaken.

Now be honest with yourself: When is the last time *your* prayer closet shook from the power of God? When did *you* change the mind of God, open spiritual eyes, or stop the rain from coming down? When was the last time you were so close to God that He decided to answer your prayers immediately? You might say, "Well, they were special." I say they weren't!

The Bible teaches that Elijah was a man just like us. In fact, Elijah was a depressed, suicidal, prideful man who gave into fear and ran for his life. Moses, writing about himself, said in Numbers 12:3, "I am the most humble man on earth." How arrogant do you have to be to write a book that proclaims you are the most humble man ever? He had an anger problem, committed murder, and was even denied access to the Promised Land because of rebellion. King David was a murdering adulterer. Peter was a power-hungry coward. Yet all these men learned one valuable lesson that took them higher than their problems and helped them overcome their negative character traits and integrity issues. They learned how to pray, and they prayed often.

I would guess that you are probably not a murdering, adulterous, depressed, suicidal megalomaniac. If you are, then this book is definitely for you. I would bet that you are naturally a better person than these men. But are you better *spiritually*? We tend to define an individual's value on their ability to impact our human world, but God places value on our willingness to become intimate with Him and our capacity to influence the spirit realm.

Are You Leading People Nowhere?

If you haven't been spending time in the secret place of prayer, then how can you hope to lead people toward freedom in Christ? If you don't have God, then what are you going to give people? At best, you will offer them a manipulated and counterfeit version of the kingdom. Why "in God's name" would we sell ourselves so far short of His best?

Chapter 2
Make Your Mark in History

The character of our praying determines the nature of our life.

—Terry Bonner

Jeff was just an ordinary man, living in a small town in Iowa. He worked at the local grocery store and attended a small Lutheran church on the weekends. Jeff was not special by any stretch of the imagination. He wasn't popular. Jeff hadn't accomplished anything special in life. He had worked at the same store for many years but wasn't concerned about doing a good job or being promoted. His philosophy in life was, "I get paid an average wage, so I will do an average job."

He attended church, but he wasn't concerned with his spiritual growth. He figured one day he would just glide into heaven. Jeff was satisfied with being just another average Christian. He was happy with just living and dying.

Late one night, Jeff was awakened by a brilliant light filling his bedroom. The light shook every fiber of his being. Slowly the light evolved and took the form of a man. The largest man he had ever seen. More light than human, he seemed to glow in all directions. He was an angel! Shocked but unafraid, Jeff just stared.

"My name is Gabriel. I have been sent by God to show you one of heaven's great mysteries." There was a flash of light, and instantly both men were floating above a great city. Thousands of people were walking, running, singing, and laughing. Gabriel said, "This is the capital city of heaven. This is where you will see what only one other man has ever seen. This is where you will gaze upon THE BOOK OF LIFE."

In what seemed like seconds, the two men had descended to the city and were walking along a beautiful street of gold. The sidewalks were made of pearl, with names etched into the flat surface. Jeff noticed that each name was made with precious jewels—diamonds, rubies, or emeralds. Some of the names he recognized, like Peter, John, and Moses, but most of the names were foreign to him.

Gabriel stated, "Those are the names of the heroes of the faith, men and women who had made a difference in life. These are people who sacrificed everything to advance the kingdom of God." The angel then pointed off into the distance and said, "Look. That is where they live."

Jeff gazed upon the most beautiful mansions he had ever seen.

Gabriel then escorted him to an open meadow, which seemed to go on forever in all directions. In the middle of the field lay a golden stand, and upon that stand lay an enormous glittering book. It was THE BOOK OF LIFE! Gabriel opened the cover and read the introduction. "In the beginning, God created the heavens and the earth!" Then chapter one started. The title of the chapter was "Adam," and the next chapter was titled "Eve." Jeff skipped ahead in the book and noticed another chapter, "Paul."

Jeff didn't quite understand what was happening, so the angel said, "Each person in history has a chapter in this book dedicated just to them." Most of the pages were worn out, dirty, smudged, and ripped. A select few were ivory white, clean, clear, and had a bright glow.

"You see, most people live their lives without regard for others. They live to please self and rarely worry about the consequences. Their battered lives are represented on these pages. A select few lived great lives, made their mark in history, and furthered the kingdom. They reached their potential and walked out their destiny. That is why their pages are white, clean, and glowing."

Jeff noticed that some of the pages were ripped out and missing.

The angel looked sad. "These pages that are ripped out are the souls who are lost for eternity," Gabriel stated. "I've read every chapter in this book. I've learned about the lives of every person who has ever lived, and I will tell you this. It is the most boring book I have ever read. Almost every chapter is dull and meaningless. Most lives seem like a waste of God's grace. Very few chapters in this book describe the kind of person that God intended them to be."

The angel then skipped ahead to a familiar-looking chapter. The title at the top of the page made Jeff's heart stop. The title read "Jeff."

Gabriel said, "So far your life has been meaningless, and you have been content with just living and dying." The angel then pointed his finger and stated, "God has destined every person to be great, but almost all have failed. What will you do with the rest of your life? Will you be great? Will you make an impact in this world? Will you reach your potential in Christ, or will you be just another boring chapter in the BOOK OF LIFE?"

There was another flash, and instantly Jeff was back in his room, sitting on his bed, surrounded by darkness, sweat pouring down his face. The last words of the angel kept racing through his mind: *Will you be just another boring chapter in the BOOK OF LIFE?*

A Life of Authority

We need to become men and women of great renown for God. The Hebrew word for *renown* is *shem*, which means *a mark of honor or authority.* You can only have this type of power by becoming a person of prayer. In the kingdom of God, beyond salvation, nothing is given—everything is earned. I know that many might disagree with this point, but the truth is that while salvation is free, kingdom authority requires effort. Do you want a better marriage, healthier relationships, or even something as simple as a greater level of peace in your life? Then action is required. If you want the type of power that can shake nations, set people free, and heal blind eyes, then you must make the effort to get on your face before God and seek Him until He gives you that power.

Making Your Mark

What is every well-known Christian in history known for? Simply put, these people made an impact for Christ. You must follow in their footsteps and become a change agent in our world. Don't settle for being average. Strive to be the most impacting Christian you can be. Make a mark in your city. Make a mark in your family!

Revelation 3:15–16 NIV: "I know your deeds, that you are neither cold nor hot. I wish you were either one or the other! So, because you are lukewarm—neither hot nor cold—I am about to spit you out of my mouth."

The Word of God Is Everything to Me

If the Word of God is worth anything, it is worth everything! It requires all that we have and all of our effort! We can't live as nominal lukewarm Christians. We are not to be indifferent to what is happening in our world. We have to be branded by fire and willing to take risks for the kingdom. A Christian who is branded by the fire of the Holy Spirit has nowhere to hide and nowhere to go. He must fight

Jesus demands 100 percent or nothing. No one has ever accomplished anything worthwhile giving only 10 percent. No person has made his or her mark in history by giving 50 percent. No, if you want to make an impression in this world for Christ, if you want to fulfill God's will for your life and reach your potential, then give 100 percent and settle for nothing less. Make your mark. Don't be average. We know from goal-setting studies that when you set the goal high and fail to reach it, you still jump higher than if you would had set the goal low and accomplished it. Don't sell yourself short and buy into the lie of the enemy that says that you will never achieve anything meaningful for God. Remember, one of the foundational truths of Christianity is Jeremiah 29:11 NIV: "I know the plans I have for you, declares the Lord, plans to prosper you and not to harm you, plans to give you hope and a future."

Wasted Time

You can work sixty hours a week or lie in bed all day, but in the end, it's all the same. It is wasted time if it's not done in some sense to propel the kingdom forward. The time that is spent is gone forever. We will never have that opportunity again. You only have so many seconds on this earth, and when your time is up, it is up. When your life is over, you will never be able to do the things you wanted to do or say the words that you wanted to say. Please don't waste your time. Make every second count.

To live a life of impact in the world, you must first live a life of impact in the secret place. A kneeling warrior of prayer can arise to accomplish great things for God. I think we have confused "great things" and "God things." Just because something is a big thing doesn't make it a God thing. It is much better to accomplish what God commands you to do and be satisfied with it, whether it is great on man's scale or seemingly insignificant. Just because something is significant or impacting doesn't necessarily make it God originated. Obedience is better than sacrifice, or so the Bible says.

CHAPTER 3

HIDDEN SECRETS: UNLOCKING TRUE PRAYER SUCCESS

To get a deep well with God, you must be schooled in the deep things of God.

—E. M. Bounds

"Put on the full armor of God, so that you will be able to stand firm against the schemes of the devil. For our struggle is not against flesh and blood, but against rulers, against the powers, against the world forces of this darkness, against the spiritual forces of wickedness in the heavenly places" (Ephesians 6:10–12 NASB).

We are in a fight to the death. This verse clearly directs us to put on the armor of God so we can fight against a real enemy. It is also evident that our enemy is not human. Rather, it is an enemy that operates in the spirit realm. Unfortunately, many new followers of Christ put on the armor and begin to do battle with anyone whom they perceive as an enemy, forgetting that our top priority is not to fight against those who are yet to believe in Christ but to lead them to an actual relationship with God. Worse are Christians who are always fighting with other followers of Christ. This type of believer on believer warfare is called NCS—New Christian Syndrome. New disciples must be taught to fire their weapons in the direction of the enemy. *Friendly fire* is a term used in modern military warfare to describe an incident where soldiers accidently shoot and kill members of their own army. Friendly fire is not acceptable in the body of Christ. Fighting against other humans is not what the armor of God was intended for. The Bible says that they (the world) will know us by our love.

Clarification point: There are people in the church who desire to live their lives in a way that is completely unbiblical. They will usually describe any correction, guidance, or disciplinary action as an attack, and they will wrongly apply this friendly-fire principle to their situations. There are times where we must be corrected in love. The correction that causes better alignment with the ways of God is beneficial for us and is not considered friendly fire. Our goal is to become more like Christ and stable enough to be corrected without being offended. Remember, human tendency is to resort to fight or flight when facing pressure. That means you either fight back or isolate and run from the issue. You must choose every day to fight to become more like Christ. Even though our struggle is not against human beings, we know the spiritual battle is carried out on the earth through people. But the origination of that battle is not human but spiritual.

Are You on the Highway to Hell?

The Bible says that we must stand firm against the strategies and tricks (*methodeia*) of the devil. *Methodeia* is a Greek word that denotes a path or roadway that is traveled over. This describes the devil's continuous attempts to secure a foothold in your thought process in order to construct a road to and through your mind. Literally a highway to hell.

The armor of God is designed to pull down strongholds and tear up this mental highway. What do these strongholds consist of? Demons, poltergeists, and vampires? No, the strongholds are our thoughts, attitudes, emotions, actions, and reactions. If we can control these areas of our minds, then we can cut off the inroads of the enemy and live in a freedom that we have never known. Science has proven it is possible to rewire your thought process and even build new roads of thinking within your mind. This is what the Bible calls renewing your mind. This is accomplished by the threefold process of daily prayer, positive biblical declaration, and meditating on the Word of God.

The Lost Armor of God

Ephesians 6:13–17 details the list of the armor that we are to symbolically put on and realistically use every day: (1) Belt of truth, (2) body armor of God's righteousness, (3) shoes of peace, (4) shield of faith, (5) helmet of salvation, and (6) sword of the Spirit, which is the Word of God. Many of us were taught to memorize this list while we were kids in Sunday school and can symbolically put it on at a moment's notice. But did you know that there are additional pieces of the armor that we have never been taught? Pieces that are described in the Bible and are vital for our success in daily warfare against the enemy. We will call them the lost armor.

1. Passion

Isaiah 59:17 describes a mantle of zeal or passion that we are to put on and live. It speaks of an apparent change of personality that results in a new level of boldness and action. This has been one of the greatest revelations in my life and has released me to live passionately for God. The Bible says to stir up the gift that is within you. We must live with energy and passion for what we are destined to do and accomplish on this planet. Learning to be passionate is one of the bedrock truths of living a successful life.

2. Long-Distance Prayer

Ephesians 6:18 NLT: "Pray in the Spirit at all times and on every occasion." This verse refers to praying in the Holy Spirit and allowing Him to guide you as you pray. Roman soldiers carried an assortment of long and short spears. Some were for throwing long distances. Others were for close combat. Each lance had its unique function and purpose. Some of our prayers are for short-distance combat and local impact. Other prayers will begin to affect nations and countries. Learn to use the spear of prayer as a powerful weapon against the enemy.

3. Vision

Ephesians 6:18 NLT: "Stay alert and be persistent in your prayers for all believers everywhere." Learn to be a watchman, with the ability to see into the darkness of this world and uncover the approaching attack of the enemy.

While standing guard duty in Sicily, I went to the armory and sign out a pair of brand-new night-vision goggles. The sailor signing out the goggles said, "If you break these glasses, you owe the government $20,000." That got my attention because I only made $298 every two weeks. Later that night, I put the goggles on and began crawling through the brush, playing soldier. Night-vision goggles locate any nearby light and amplify it to the point that you can see in the dark. Isn't that amazing? The ability to look into the darkness and locate a small amount of redeemable light. As followers of Christ, we need to be skilled enough to look deep into the darkness of our communities and search for the lost lights (hurting people) and amplify them through encouragement. Many of the rejected souls in our community are actually redeemable lights that could easily be transformed into mighty explosions of God light if given a chance. Daily prayer will help us see people as God sees them. Lack of prayer allows our filters to become darkened, which results in us seeing others through the lens of religion rather than the lens of authentic grace.

Interesting fact: Can looking at a bright light with night-vision goggles cause blindness? If Christians are described as being a light to the world, then we need to be careful we are not overly peering into the lives of other Christians, looking for mistakes or errors. People who practice prayer are often called *watchmen*. Watchmen were intended to peer into the darkness to look for the enemy.

In the Spirit realm, we are spiritual policemen, and we are to develop a strong desire to do good. In prayer, we can begin to spot and decipher the plans of the enemy. We identify the strategies of hell that have been designed to wreak havoc on our communities and families. We then take that information and begin to arrest the spiritual powers behind that attack and release the victims who have been held captive. We do this primarily through the vehicle of daily prayer.

4. Boldness

Ephesians 6:19 NLT: "And pray for me, too. Ask God to give me the right words so I can boldly explain God's mysterious plan that the Good News is for the Jews and Gentiles alike. I am in chains now, still preaching this message as God's ambassador. So pray that I will keep on speaking boldly for him, as I should."

According to the Bible, we are to live and speak with a boldness that resembles the courage of a lion. Lions trot in with a victory roar that alerts all that the king of the jungle has arrived. We are to live bold lives that are filled with the victorious sound of the kingdom. Our very presence should alert our communities that the King is here and that we are His representatives in this world. It is time to guard our mouths and to be careful what we speak. Our words accomplish something powerful as we declare them. Whether that impact is good or bad depends on what we are saying. Our words can open doors to hell or doors to heaven in our communities. If there is any question about what we are to say, then remember the Bible says to speak the very words of God. To speak what God would speak. Sometimes it is better to not speak at all and simply live out the kingdom principles of the Bible. But when you do speak, let it be with courage, boldness, grace, and positivity.

Pray in the Spirit at all times and on every occasion. Stay alert and be persistent in your prayers for all believers everywhere. And pray for me, too. Ask God to give me the right words so I can boldly explain God's mysterious plan that the Good News is for the Jews and Gentiles alike. I am in chains now, still preaching this message as God's ambassador. So pray that I will keep on speaking boldly for him, as I should." (Ephesians 6:18–20 NLT)

God's Drive-Through Armor Wash

In the Vietnam War, many M-16 rifles would not fire correctly. The reason was simple. They were so sensitive that even a little dirt would cause them to malfunction. I have a 300 Savage hunting rifle, and one day I walked deep into the woods to fire the gun and get ready for hunting season. I hadn't cleaned the weapon for many years, and it was filthy. I loaded it and pulled the trigger, but nothing happened. It wouldn't fire due to the amount of dirt inside the trigger mechanism. After a thorough cleaning, I reloaded the rifle and pulled the trigger, and a deafening roar quickly followed. It fired correctly because it was clean.

How about your armor? Is it being maintained? Is it working correctly? Or has it been neglected and misused? Maybe you have the armor, and it hasn't been used at all.

Spiritual Armor Durability Test

Are you easily offended? Do you tend to gossip or speak negatively? Do you malfunction at the first sign of spiritual warfare? If you answered yes, then you must quickly take your armor through God's drive-through armor wash. Clean it, wear it, and use it.

- ☐ Repentance washes it.
- ☐ You wear it.
- ☐ Through prayer you use it.

CHAPTER 4

VALUABLE LESSONS ON THE JOURNEY OF PRAYER

We need to be set aflame and empowered by the fiery energy of a fiery soul.

—E. M. Bounds

I love the thought of finding hidden treasure. As a kid, I loved watching old pirate movies. You know the ones—where they dig up the treasure chest, dust off the sand, and slowly open the top. The pirate would scoop up a handful of red rubies, green emeralds, and diamonds of every color imaginable. I used to think I could find treasure by digging in the backyard of our home in Idaho. As an eight-year-old, I did not understand that finding hidden treasure required much effort. More effort than I was willing to exert. I was searching for that sense of wonder and amazement that arises when you find something of value.

Have you ever stumbled upon a fantastic idea? In this chapter, we will search for life lessons that are hiding in plain sight. We will dig for jewels of prayer revelation. I have learned many valuable lessons on this journey of prayer. Actually, I stumbled upon these revelations as I practiced my daily prayer habit. I use the word *practice* for a reason. I know there is a cringe factor when I connect the word *practice* to *prayer*. My intention is to create a basic understanding of the foundation of prayer. Successful prayer is established by committed discipline, and that requires practice. There is an old soccer phrase that says, "Practice doesn't make perfect—it makes permanent." If you practice bad habits day after day, you will cement those bad habits and will not improve. If you practice good habits, then you will permanently establish them in your life, and you will see steady and measurable growth. Genuine improvement comes from combining disciplined practice with knowledge of your topic. In this case, the topic is prayer.

When Does a Lesson Become Revelation?

A lesson is something you learn, and it may or may not actually change you. A revelation is a lesson that you learn and then live out in your daily life. These revelations have changed my life and have catapulted my spiritual man into a deeper intimacy with God.

I didn't find these principles at Walmart. I didn't learn them from a self-help book. Nor did I receive them from a supernatural dream. I learned these principles the hard way. I had to make a conscious decision to get on my face before God every single day. There are no magic bullets in life. If you want to fix your issues and solve your problems, then you are going to have to do something about them. You can't fix your problems by attending a conference or by a gifted person praying over you. God, at times, does answer our prayers supernaturally and immediately. But that does not give us the right to avoid disciplined prayer. Lasting change is rarely experienced by those who have an "I want it now" mentality.

Learning to communicate with God is like digging in a field that has been overrun with weeds. A weed is a valueless plant growing wild, especially one that grows on cultivated ground to the injury of the desired crop (Dictionary.com). Weeds symbolize areas of your life that are detrimental to your true spiritual growth. They are habits or actions that will take root and destroy the healthy ground that is required for biblical discipleship. You must spend time in the field digging through the weeds and tilling the hard soil. The digging process is praying, and praying often. The more I dug in prayer, the more I learned about prayer.

It was like digging through dirt to find a buried diamond. As you dig, you begin to see the outline of a smudged object buried deep in the soil. The closer you get to the object, the more enticing it becomes. With your eyes, it appears to be an ordinary stone. But you know something of value is right beneath the obvious. A sense of wonder and amazement arises because you have found something intriguing. As you dig around this object (more prayer), you begin to clear away the dirt of confusion, and you gain spiritual clarity. Now your desire and passion to dig have caught up with your level of wonder and amazement. You dig harder and faster to once and for all uncover this dirty stone and bring it to the surface.

Finally, you hold this desired object in your hands. You begin to wipe away the dirt and wash away the mud, and you see a glimmer of beauty emerge. You can't sleep, because your imagination is running wild. You scrub this stone until the muddy object becomes a beautiful, shiny diamond.

What did you learn in this process? You learned that digging is more than putting your hands in the ground and moving your fingers around. Sadly, most Christians believe that praying is a mind-numbing religious duty. They rarely pray, and if they do, it is only a halfhearted attempt to satisfy their nagging sense of guilt. They are dabbling in prayer, when what is needed is a commitment to hard work. A disciplined prayer strategy that creates a divine connection with God. You find these prayer revelations by digging deep. Shallow Christianity has never uncovered the deep things of God. You bring them to the surface by praying with more strategy and discipline. The object is revealed to be a diamond by meticulous care and hard work.

Praying with better understanding, strategy, and passion will cause us to operate in the type of prayer that will impact our worlds and change our situations. Here are a few of the prayer jewels that I uncovered while digging in the desert of God's presence. I use the word *desert* because many people feel like they are in a spiritual wilderness when they are praying. I would say that water found in the wilderness tastes better than water purchased at the supermarket. Why? You are thirstier when you are lost in the wilderness. A man walking through a grocery store might buy a bottle of water only to throw half of it away. While a man lost in the desert tends to savor every last drop of the water he finds. If you are in the desert phase of your life, then celebrate, because you will soon enjoy the satisfying water of the Holy Spirit as you pray.

We are dying of spiritual thirst because we are living in the wilderness of nonprayer. It is time to stir our passions and become desperate in our journeys toward God. I pray these revelations will sink deep into your soul and allow you to rise to new heights in the Spirit of God. Here are thirteen lessons that have become bedrock truths in my life:

1. Changing your atmosphere will change the way people see you

Your church and/or home has a spiritual atmosphere. As a calling card, that describes who and what you are. Your atmosphere is only a reflection of what has been going on in your situation over a period of time. You can change this environment by changing your habits and actions. Inactive prayer allows the atmosphere to reflect what has been or what the enemy would like it to be. Proactive prayer takes the initiative and causes the atmosphere to reflect what God has destined it to be.

Your atmosphere must incite people to real kingdom praying, not into a false sense of security. You must break the stranglehold of religion from around the neck of the body of Christ and release the warriors to take up the mantle of war once again. Are you choking on spiritual air tainted with the smog of prayerlessness and church politics? Change your prayer habits, and you will change your atmosphere. Change your atmosphere, and you will change your life. In doing this you will

- have success in prayer,
- restore the dry areas in your life, and
- find that answered prayers become commonplace.

God's presence doesn't magically appear because we play the right music or chant our Christian code words. We must cultivate the atmosphere of God's presence. The power of expectation is the best way for you to birth change in your life or family. Expect God to show up and expect great things. What you expect, you will speak, and what you speak, you will become.

2. Are you leading or loning?

Urban Dictionary defines *loning* as being in a crowd in which no one is paying attention to you. Are you a leader or a loner? Are you leading the pack or following the crowd? I have always encouraged my interns and staff to follow hard after my example. The Bible teaches that we are to follow others as they follow Christ. Every great athlete knows that you will play to the level of your competition. I played tennis in high school, college, and in tournaments across the Northwest. I can tell you that when I played against a weaker opponent, my game suffered. I literally played down to my opponent's level, and I made fundamental mistakes in strategy. On the other hand, your level of skill rises when you play against better opponents. This approach can also be applied to the art of prayer.

If my staff and interns are great prayer warriors, then my prayer level will rise to greater heights. When they are nipping at my heels, then it is time for me to up the ante and pray better and more often. I want them to succeed, not fail. When they succeed in prayer, I succeed in prayer.

3. Your ability to follow God is connected to your ability to hear his voice

Let me ask you a question: Are you ahead of God or trailing far behind? Most people would say they are lagging far behind. Why? Because we do not really believe that we can be close to God. We label those who claim to have an intimate relationship with God as arrogant. In our pride, we try to give them a healthy dose of humility. In a weird way, we are trying to bring people down to our level rather than lifting ourselves up to God's level. After all, God is God, and we are mere humans. Here is a question: Are we trying to build the church by cracking the whip of condemnation and guilt?

Let me explain. The Bible says the children of Israel camped in the wilderness, and they only moved when God moved. How did they know when to move? The Old Testament describes the presence of God as a pillar of fire by night and a cloud by day. The physical presence of God hovered over the camp. When the cloud shifted, they rose up and moved as well. When the cloud was not moving, the people remained where they were.

The church has not been good at realizing when the shift of God's Spirit is in motion. We tend to ignore the moving of the cloud and dig our roots deeper into the sand of what we know, or I should say, what we are comfortable with. We can get so comfortable with the status quo that we forget that God is rarely stationary for very long. People will say, "What we are doing is good! Why change it?" Always remember, good is the enemy of best when it comes to prayer.

The aim of kingdom life is to move with God. You shouldn't have to conduct a straw poll to see if it is politically expedient to move ahead. Some people are not okay with leaving their comfort zones to venture out into the unknown of God's will. You must learn to recognize God's voice and be able to make sound biblical decisions. What is God saying and where is He leading?

I am sure the children of Israel were not overjoyed at the prospect of getting up early, packing up the whole camp, and moving twenty miles just because a leader felt that a particular cumulous cloud had been supernaturally moved by the Spirit of the Lord. I have often felt like Moses. I have stood in front of a church and told them that "the cloud of God is moving, and it is time to shift into what He is doing." I said it with confidence. I knew God had spoken to me, yet the people had the famous spiritual deer-in-the-headlights look. Don't be dismayed. Leaders are to lead! They are not to wallow in a false sense of comfort because a majority of people agree with their decisions. Several times, my wife and I moved our family to a new state because we felt God had called us to follow the cloud. This included changing jobs, leaving friends, and selling most of our possessions. It wasn't easy, but it was God. We are not called to *easy*. We are called to do the will of God in our lives.

Can you discern when the cloud is moving and when it is not? God's will is for you to go with Him and be His intimate friend. He never intended for you to watch the show from a safe distance. We spend too much time trying to negotiate our way through life like blind men crossing the road, afraid of every sound and only moving after bumping into a brick wall. God's plan is for us to spend time in prayer, hear His clear command, and negotiate our way through life. Then and only then will we reflect the life of Christ, when He said, "I only do what I see my Father do."

4. Increase your value by increasing your intimacy

A friend of mine called to tell me that he was getting fired from his job as a youth pastor. He said, "I am sorry that I disappointed you." I replied, "You did not disappoint me, because our friendship is not based on your job performance." It is the same with God. He values you because He loves you, not because of what you can do for Him. That being said, you need to understand that you can increase your value with God through increased intimacy with Him.

Example: My son appreciates me because I spend time with him. What if I completely ignore my son? Would he still love me and value me as a father? Yes, but not to the same degree that he would if our relationship was great. That is the nature of relationships. Ongoing dialogue and interaction. The disease of neglect will always seek to destroy your relationship with God. A neglected relationship leads to divorce. We do not want to be divorced from the Lord. The Bible says your spiritual gift is without repentance even if you are. That means that you can still operate in your gifting without a real relationship with God.

Explanation: The Bible says that we are given gifts or talents that we can use to impact this world. The gifts are without repentance, which means that God gives them and will not usually take them away. We can be operating in our gifting (preaching, worship, prayer, etc.) and still be living in sin, offense, and unforgiveness. Please be warned—believing that your value in life and in God comes from your gifting and talent will lead to impending spiritual doom. Many people in the church think that using their gifts in public causes others to value them. That is a human way of thinking and acting. Know this—God will never place value on you because of your gifting alone!

It is true that we increase the capacity to be great at our talents by honing our crafts daily. It is also true that kingdom impact is based on your ability to improve your gifting and apply it in the real world. But never confuse kingdom impact with intimacy with God.

5. Secret victory leads to public impact

Real impact in the natural realm must first be won through prayer in the spiritual realm. The road to success is paved in the secret place of your prayer closet. Miracles are birthed in the spirit realm and then reflected in the human realm. Jesus was the greatest example of a person who walked out this principle. He got up early in the morning and prayed on a mountain. Then he performed miracles in the afternoon. His success wasn't in the miracle; it was in the secret place prayer.

6. Today's pain is tomorrow's victory

The Bible teaches that Jesus was in a garden praying on the night He was arrested. He was then taken to prison, convicted, and crucified. His death gave us freedom over sin and access to heaven.

Jesus prayed the victory in the garden long before He was nailed to the cross. We sing beautiful hymns about the garden as if it were a place of soaking and meditation. These songs imply that Jesus was a patient man waiting for His destiny to unfold. The truth is, the garden was a hard place. It was the place Jesus prayed all night by himself, while others slept. Where His prayers were so intense and passionate that He began to bleed. It was also the place where His disciples denied Him and ran away as the guards arrested him.

Great victories require time in your garden, where you may be deserted and discredited. Where the fear and worry of life's circumstances so overwhelm you that you begin to bleed spiritually. As Jesus was dying on the cross, he turned to a thief who was being crucified on a nearby post, and Jesus said in Luke 23:43 NLT, "I assure you, today, you will be with me in paradise." Jesus was able to say this because He first earned the spiritual victory in the garden of pain. Our greatest verbal declarations are always based on the passion and fire of desperate prayer.

7. Are you dead or alive?

Jeremiah 20:9 NLT: "But if I say I'll never mention the Lord or speak in his name, his word burns in my heart like a fire. It's like a fire in my bones! I am worn out trying to hold it in! I can't do it!" I need to be branded by fire and full of passion. When I am on fire for God, I will change a generation and a community. If it does not burn in you, it won't burn in them. A great preacher once said, "I set myself on fire, and people come to see me burn." If your community is not changed by your life, then maybe you need to be set on fire spiritually. Your passion can ignite those around you into a firestorm of God chasers and world changers.

Many Christians in history were killed for their beliefs. They were burned at the stake for their dedication to Jesus Christ. I can honor their sacrifices by burning spiritually for Christ today. By being passionate and alive with the joy of God in my heart. Their sacrifices were not wasted as long as I live passionately for Christ today.

8. Remove labels of limitation

We need to eliminate the tag of *intercessor* from individuals and place it upon the church body as a whole. The decline in personal prayer is fostered by the idea that only a handful of people in the church have the gift of prayer. That only a small team of dedicated prayer ladies have the ability to connect with God. The Bible declares in Matthew 21:13 AMP, "My house shall be called a house of prayer." Jesus did not say His house would be a house of preaching and worship. He never declared that His house would be a house of a few intercessors. No! He proclaimed that His church would be a house that prayed. There is no such thing as the office of intercession. The Bible has never taught that intercession is for a select group of chosen ones. Prayer is the job of every disciple. I do believe that you can increase your capacity for intercession, and thereby increase your effectiveness in prayer. Remember, you get out of prayer what you put into it.

9. Life changes when God shows up suddenly

The idea is that God will suddenly cause things to change in your life. These changes will propel you into the next stage of your destiny. This caused me to pray with greater passion and frequency. I believe that through prayer, the answer to my problem is just around the corner. I may not see it yet, but it is coming. The Bible declares that God's word does not go out and then return empty. It says that it will accomplish what God desires, and it will achieve the purpose for which it was sent (Isaiah 55:11). So as I pray and God speaks, I know that the answer or the "suddenly" is just around the corner

I love the story of Daniel's suddenly recorded in Daniel 10. He was passionately praying for his nation, and God heard his prayer. The Bible says that God answered Daniel's prayer the moment he thought about praying. Imagine that. The moment you think about your prayer, the answer is on the way. In this story, we find that even though the answer was a suddenly, it still took twenty-one days of additional praying to actually arrive. Sometimes our suddenly is sudden and sometimes it is subtle. Either way, God answers prayers.

Twenty-five years ago I encountered my first suddenly. I found myself standing on a porch staring at the sky, desperately praying for a miracle. I was a young pastor making around $13,000 a year. I received a letter from the IRS saying that I owed $2,000 immediately. This was back in the days when the IRS would actually come after you if you owed it money. This was very serious. I had no money and no natural way of coming up with $2,000. I stared at the ground and prayed, "God, if you are really there, I need a sign. I am going to turn around and point my finger to the sky, and I want to see a shooting star right where I point. This is my test to prove that you are real and you will help me."

I flipped around, pointed, and guess what? Yep, a shooting star exploded across the sky right where I pointed my finger. It was God reassuring me that He was actually alive and willing to help. The next morning, I received a letter in the mail from a relative in another state who was giving to the church for the first time. They didn't go to church, so they sent the money to the only real Christian they knew. Me! The check was for $2,000. The exact amount I needed to pay off the IRS. The amazing part of this story is the fact that the letter was sent two weeks earlier. Long before I even knew that I owed the money. God knew two weeks earlier that I would be praying. He orchestrated not only a letter and check to be sent, but He caused a star to pass by at the exact time of my greatest need. The wise men followed a star to Jesus, and I followed a star to my answered prayer.

10. Do not forge God's signature on your opinion

When I was in high school, I forged my father's signature. I had misbehaved in school, and the principal assigned me to Saturday detention. The school also mailed a letter to my parents, which needed to be signed and returned. I intercepted the letter at the post office and forged my father's signature and mailed it back. I then told my father that my friend and I were going to ride our bikes to the next town and would be gone all day. My dad knew something was up, called the school, and my cover was blown. It does not pay to forge a signature because, in the end, it is not real. Everything gained by the forgery is built on a lie. When we say something is from God and it isn't, we are committing spiritual fraud by assigning God's name and authority to our opinion or desire.

Not every idea, opinion, or nugget of knowledge that drops into your mind is of God. It is easy to speak your own opinion and declare it as a word from the Lord, but is that really true? Do not say something is from God unless He has indeed spoken it to you.

The fear of God should cause us to talk less and pray more.

Sometimes we are in love with the sounds of our own voices. So we become addicted to speaking on behalf of God. The danger lies in saying a word is from God when in reality it is only your opinion. This is a form a manipulation and control. I want a real word from God, not a human opinion tainted by offense, filtered by experience, and falsely covered with a "Thus saith the Lord." I want a heavenly word and have set my face to seek God until I get one. Living off of opinions is like carrying around fool's gold. It looks good, but it isn't worth anything. A prophetic word might sound great and even be enticing to the soul, but is it a valid word from heaven? God told my wife that I was the man she would marry. She never told me. She didn't use the manipulation card of "God said we would marry." She quietly prayed until God arranged the circumstances that led to our marriage.

11. Declaring truth destroys negativity

This has been the most impacting truth that I have known. There is a reason I named this book *Declare* and not *Worry*, even though the word *worry* best describes most churches or individuals today. I love to declare and pray the Word of God out loud. Declaring the Word of God breaks down the stronghold of negativity in our lives. My human words can be filled with fear and worry, but proclaiming the Word of God initiates a spiritual principle. Isaiah 55:11 NLT: "It is the same with my word. I send it out, and it always produces fruit. It will accomplish all I want it to, and it will prosper everywhere I send it." Remember, negative words *negate* the promises of God in your life. This is our best method for combating the enemy when it comes to our conversations. How do you deal with a person who is always using his or her spare time to gossip and complain? The antidote to gossip is to use your tongue to speak about God and declare the great things of His kingdom. We must come against the enemy in the opposite spirit that he has attacked you.

12. Writing heals our hearts and soothes our spirits

Malachi 3:16 teaches that God records our spiritual conversations (God talk) in a heavenly journal. He actually has our conversations about Him written down. What does that tell you about how much God cares for us? He is so in tune with our lives and so invested in what we do that He writes down our conversations. This should give us some pause when we are speaking with others.

I am a big proponent of daily journaling. If God likes to journal, then so do I. It is an amazing way to record our authentic feelings and our real-world situations. Journaling is like God's counseling appointment. It is where we are honest about our life, and it gives us an opportunity to change. Journaling gives me a correct appraisal of my day and my emotional status. It goes hand and hand with meditation and contemplation.

13. Focusing on God results in true life change

Kabod is the biblical word that describes the weighty presence of

God. It means to have the power to act or influence. For too long we have been enamored by the manifestations that can occur in the presence of God. We will say things like, "Did you feel God's presence? Wasn't it beautiful?" But we have failed to understand that the presence of God is for impact and the power to change. It is not so we can say that we had a powerful manifestation of God.

Let's be honest! Why do most churches seek great manifestations? So we can get in *Charisma* magazine or on Christian television. So thousands of people will flock to our churches from all over the world, and people will declare us the next great revival hot spot? Why do individuals want to have a great *Kabod* experience? Many times it is so they can find value and, in some cases, prove their spiritual superiority. These reasons only reveal the shallowness of our Christianity and should cause us to rethink our current definition of the presence of God.

God intended for us to experience the *Kabod* of His presence so we can have the power to act and influence our society. I wish all the angelic visitations, prophetic words, and supernatural experiences had at least an equal measure of life change.

U.S. News & World Report declared that churches are twenty-sixth on the list of the most influential factors in society. I don't want to be the least impacting force in my community. I believe the kingdom of God should be the number one trigger for life change in our cities. This will only happen when we experience the real presence of God. Let your prayers be fueled by the desire to experience more of Him.

CHAPTER 5

TURNING YOUR WASTELAND INTO DESTINY

People who are great thinkers and great students must become great prayers.
—E. M. Bounds

Where am I now, this desert is so familiar.
This loneliness has scarred me before,
Is this where you found, or is this
Where you have brought me?
Your voice no longer can I ignore
My heart lies in pieces.
Please pick me up and put me
Back together again like only You can.
Abba, like water to this soul
Abba, I need you because I got nowhere else to go.
Is that You there, whispering so softly
Calming all the madness inside.
In your sanctuary is where I want to be
For this desperate heart has found no better place
to be
Then to be found in You.
—Jason Morant ("Abba" from the *Open* CD)

What a powerful song! It describes what many people feel as they play out their existence on earth. Lonely, scared, and broken. God loves to rescue people whose lives are nothing more than shattered pieces of hope spread out across the floor of life. He has such a wonderful way of gathering those broken pieces and fusing them back together. God never restores you to what you were, but always to something greater, stronger, and better.

Every Outcast Needs a Home

Life is filled with hurting people. The depressed, suicidal, and addicted fill our communities, but they don't always fill our churches. Why? Because the religious are not usually the first to embrace those who are walking through tough times. Are you reaching out to those in your community who were rejected by the church and shunned by society? People with broken marriages, drug problems, and depression. Sunday school misfits, religious rejects, and wrong-side-of-the-tracks city dwellers.

David was one of my favorite Old Testament characters. As a boy, he worked as a shepherd. He spent many nights on a mountainside, gazing at the stars and contemplating life. It was here that he developed the heart of worship that later led him to serve as an adviser and leader for King Saul. Saul suffered from bouts of depression and anger. At times he became jealous of David and even tried to kill him. It was during these bouts of anger that David would retreat to the safety of a wilderness cave, the Cave of Adullam. No doubt he longed for the isolation and anonymity of the hillside once more.

The Bible says that people who were outcast, depressed, and poor would gather with David in the cave. An army of misfits that would eventually lead the greatest army in the world. The worst of the worst came knocking on his door (or side of the cave). It seemed like David had the "worse" anointing. Every person who showed up to help him was worse than the last guy. It was literally a vagabond group of losers (world's term) who saw in David what he could not see in himself. They saw hope, redemption, and a future. We are the modern-day Davids, and our churches are the modern-day Caves of Adullam. The hurting people in our communities will come knocking when they realize we are safe havens of hope. They will join our crusade to impact this world for God.

Daniel 7:25 AMP: "Wear down the saints of the Most High." We aren't always excited and joyful. We can often get worn down physically and spiritually as we travel through life. I believe God allows us to be worn out to reduce us to one focus...Him! He wants to bring us back to the simplicity and purity of daily communication with Jesus. There is no way around the desert. Moses brought Israel out of Egypt and wanted to travel around the desert and straight into the Promised Land. But God had other ideas. He ordered them straight into the wilderness to learn the concept of intimate communication with Him.

What Are Dry Times?

They are a period in our lives when we no longer feel God's presence or hear His voice. Times when His guidance and direction seem far from us. Listen—if God is not talking, there is a reason and a purpose. The reason is usually our fault (lack of prayer, sin in our lives, comfort zones). The purpose is His doing. Often, He wants to teach us a principle, and He will always teach us in a way that will bring us closer to Him. At times, God's methods are straightforward and fair. On other occasions they may seem harsh and unfair. One thing I know to be absolutely true about God is this: He will never force me to communicate with Him. He may arrange circumstances and situations to bring me closer to the kingdom. But if I am not listening, He may just quit speaking until I realize I have a spiritual problem. Actually, God is always speaking to us. We are the ones who cut off the communication and refuse to hear His voice. Get past the dry spell by finding a quiet place and just listen. Listen for the still, small voice of God.

The Intersection Game

Have you ever played the intersection game? Here's how it goes: I would be driving a van full of kids across town, and I would wait until they were completely focused on talking with each other. I would stop at an intersection, and if no one was behind me, I would just wait. Sometimes we were there for more than two minutes before someone noticed. "Hey, why aren't we moving?" How many times has God stopped at the intersection of our lives, waiting for us to realize that we aren't moving? We are not moving because we are not paying attention to the real driver of our lives, Jesus Christ.

Journey to the Deep Things of God

Elijah went to Mount Horeb to be anointed a prophet. Moses went to Mount Horeb to become a great leader. Horeb literally means *desolation* and represents the desolate, dry times in our lives. Like Elijah, you need to become the best prophet in your own life. This can only happen when you have been tested in the sweltering heat of desert experiences. To become a great leader like Moses, we must learn to climb Mount Horeb and pray from the mountain. The mountain has always symbolized the presence of God. It also represents the physical location where you pray. The Bible says that God inhabits the places we dedicate as our prayer rooms. The places we choose to worship and pray. The climb represents the prayer journey that gets us to the top of the mountain and deep into the heart of God.

Two Reasons why we go through the dry times:
- Lack of intimacy with God
- God wants to teach us something

Lessons learned in the desert:
1. You will learn to embrace the desert time, and you will accept the lessons that God is teaching you there.
2. The strength and character that you develop in the desert times will get you through any situation you may encounter in life.

Your Desolation Is Your Preparation for Promotion

In the story of Moses leading the people of Israel out of slavery in Egypt, we see something interesting. They were driven into the desert to learn a new mind-set about God. Unfortunately, they could not get past their victim mentality. So they were required to stay in the wilderness until a generation died out. God was actually allowing them time to teach the next generation how to view the world through God's eyes. Israel had to go another round in the desert because they would not allow their lives to be changed. The sooner we learn what God is teaching, the faster we will progress to the next season of our lives. Here is some good advice. Don't escape the desert season too early. You might miss some valuable lessons. Don't stay in the desert too long. You might not survive.

God Will Never Allow You to Be Promoted to Your Promised Land until You Are Changed by the Lessons You Embrace in Your Desert

Let's be clear about this point. The desert should never be your permanent dwelling place. Learning your desert lessons leads to promotion and eventually to freedom. D. L. Moody said, "Lighthouses blow no horns; they just shine" (quotation taken from YouthDownSouth.Org). We need to shine with the glory of God like Moses coming out of the Tent of Meeting. It needs to be evident to all that we have been spending time with God in the desert. If your prayer life seems dry and empty, then you need to implement the following steps and experiment with prayer.

Three-Week Prayer Challenge

An *experiment* is an act or operation for the purpose of discovering something unknown. It is for testing a principle. In this experiment, we are learning something new in prayer, and we are testing these biblical principles to see if they actually work.

1. Three-week prayer challenge: Choose a three-week period (starting today). Twenty-one days is an attainable goal and will be long enough to create a habit of prayer in your life.

Set a goal for how many minutes you will spend in prayer and Bible meditation.

2. Quiet Reflection: Your prayer times should be marked by moments of quiet reflection. This will help you to slow down and get your mind and emotions in check.

3. Prayer Books: Reading a book on prayer is one of the quickest ways to get inspired. Inspired people become motivated. Motivated people will pray.

4. Practice PRAY 7/3—7 Days a week and 3 times a day should bring your life to a complete halt. Spend several minutes acknowledging God's presence in your life. This will bring you into spiritual focus and allow you to refresh your emotions and physical body.

CHAPTER 6

VISIONS OF GREATNESS DANCING
THROUGH MY HEAD

The deep things of God have never been studied. They have
been prayed.

—E. M. Bounds

Visions of greatness lead to self-glory. The worship of self is the
primary way to destroy our pursuit of God. Daily prayer will help
you place God at the pinnacle of your life. This will by its very
nature remove you from the top shelf. One of the first lessons that
every struggling prayer warrior must learn is the need to kill the
visions of grandeur that float through our minds. We must strive
to be great for God and make significant impacts in the world. We
must do so in a way that does not steal glory from God. After all,
whose kingdom are we serving, His or ours? How many business
cards have we seen with the words *apostle, bishop,* or *Dr.,* and
for the highly anointed, it might include all three. When will our
business cards reflect our real mission—prayer? Sure, it doesn't
flow off the tongue quite as well as the term "Most highly esteemed
bishop of Seattle." But it accurately describes our actual function
in this world: prayer.

Sometimes my life seems like a circus. Filled with amazing
stories of living life without prayer. Here are a few dramatic
stories from my not-so-distant past. These tales are true and not
exaggerated. They are not fairy tales from some far-off land. No,
they have happened and could happen again in any church. Great
stories from the circus tent—hope you enjoy, but please don't try
this at home.

Story 1: Becoming a Legend—the Worship of Self

I witnessed a partial miracle at a conference several years ago. It was a genuine miracle. I was exactly two feet from the person receiving prayer, and I was assisting the evangelist as she prayed. The problem started several months later when the evangelist began to testify about this miracle. Her testimony included several exaggerated points. Not a lot, but enough to raise a red flag. The next year at another conference, the story was even bigger, and as the years went by, the story has now become legend. Too bad it's only a legend in the evangelist's mind. If you exaggerate your ministry to help the cause of Christ, you too will become a legend in your own mind.

Story 2: The Demon-Buster Gets Busted

My first encounter with the demonic was also the first time I realized that my spiritual power was more theory and self-proclamation than it was actual kingdom authority. The place: western Alaska. A knock on the door would change my spiritual life forever. I went to the front door of the parsonage to see who could be knocking at such a late hour. It was one of my deacons, informing me that a local girl was demon possessed and in need of deliverance. I didn't believe him at first. I mean really, a demon possessed girl? Sure I watched *The Exorcist* like every other kid in the '80s. But I didn't recall ever taking a class in Bible college on demonology. They taught us to memorize the books of the Bible and how to organize a potluck, but never how to deal with a demon-possessed thirteen-year-old. Looking back, that might have been helpful. The deacon showed me his hand, which was bleeding. Evidently, the girl bit him as he tried to pray for her. I guessed this was going to require assistance a little higher than deacon level.

"Wow, this is going to be cool. My own personal exorcism." I wasn't looking to become demon fodder. I thought casting out a demon might bring some much-needed advertisement to our complacent little church. I just hoped I would fare better than the

Catholic priest in the movie. Little did I know, this one encounter would shock me into realizing my lack of real authority and place me firmly on the path of searching for God's true power.

I drove across town and located the girl's house. I remember getting out of the vehicle and hearing the howl of a man's voice coming from inside. The atmosphere was ripe with fear. I completely understood that whatever was in that house was not from heaven or earth, and that left only one place...hell. The hair on the back of my neck stood up, and I knew I was in big trouble. The great demon-buster was about to get busted, and it was too late to leave now. No way to escape and save face. The gig was up, and I had to go in and face the demon.

An evangelist from down south was staying at the parsonage with me, and I had asked him to accompany me on this great adventure. He was in town to conduct a marriage seminar. Since the intermingling of a man and a woman in the relationship of marriage could sometimes resemble an exorcism, he was perfect for the job.

We entered the house and were shocked at what we saw. A thirteen-year-old girl lying on the floor, with four adults pinning her down. Her younger brother stood crying in the corner, so I took him to the kitchen and sat him in a chair. I gave him my new Spirit-Filled Life Bible. I told him that there was magic power in this book, and no harm would come to him. He grabbed the Bible and held it to his face, sobbing. I slowly understood a powerful truth: God doesn't want to just be in a Bible. He intends to live in our hearts, and He wants intimacy with us. God was in my heart, but we weren't intimate. I am not a prophet, but I could already see how this night was going to end, and it wasn't pretty.

This young girl was skinny, and it amazed me to see a girl of such small stature fighting four grown adults. Yet she struggled to get free, so I grabbed one arm while my friend, the marriage expert, grabbed the other. The girl's head spun toward my friend, and she stated in a deep, guttural voice, like you might hear in a horror movie, "What are you doing here?" This one statement said it all. The power of God in the marriage-seminar guy was evident and clearly seen by this demon. The girl then flung her head toward me and tried to take a chunk out of my arm. The demon didn't say a word and didn't have to. The demonic look in the eyes of that young girl revealed the truth. I had no power, the demon knew it, and he was about to have roast pastor for dinner.

For the next four hours, we engaged in a verbal battle with this demon. I used phrases I had heard in other exorcism stories, like "Say *Jesus* now and be free," to which the demon replied, "*No.*" I even commanded the demon to fly back to hell, where he came from. I was confident that was something a Catholic priest would have said, and after all, they were the experts on this sort of thing. But it only resulted in the demon once again trying to take a chunk out of my arm. Well, that didn't work. I realized God was using these four hours to show me my lack of intimacy with Him. At one point, the girl and the demon were shoved to the back of my mind, and all I could see before me was my lack of Christ.

In the wee hours of the morning, the girl finally calmed down and fell asleep. Her parents, local pastors, asked us to come into the kitchen for a cup of coffee. I was pretty confident that whatever we were doing was not over yet, but my addiction to caffeine overruled my logic. Within moments I heard the pitter-patter of feet running down the hallway. My old law enforcement days kicked in, and I ran after her. The girl had locked herself in the bathroom. I could see through the keyhole that she had a knife in one hand and pills in the other. I was afraid she would kill herself, so I kicked down the door and wrapped my arms around her. For the next hour, we continued our back-and-forth verbal jousting to no avail. Eventually, the night ended, and I drove home. Defeated! I left that house feeling scared and realizing that I had just encountered pure evil. I looked deep into the recess of my own heart, and I didn't like what I was seeing. I didn't sleep at all that night. In fact, I turned all the lights on in the house. I sat at the kitchen table reading from my Spirit-Filled Life Bible. I figured if I wasn't spiritual, at least my Bible was. So much for my career as a traveling exorcist.

Story 3: The Who's Who of the Charismatic Zoo

I love going to the zoo in Seattle. I watch the semiconscious animals grovel for food and entertain the masses. My favorite is the ferocious lion of Africa, who has been turned into a domesticated house cat. The zoo gives me a small glimpse of what life might be like in some far-off land. Yet it still reminds me that I live in a predictable and safe environment void of any real adventure.

I think the church can be like a zoo sometimes. We flock to conferences to hear the who's who tells us about the zoo (church). Then we go home excited yet still living in our safe and predictable lives. We need to understand that to be important in the kingdom of God, we must become great in the arena of prayer. I wonder if famous evangelists and preachers ever get sick of being the domesticated house cats entertaining the masses for money. May God create a new breed of pastor, men and women willing to speak the truth of God's kingdom without fearing what man will say. It is easy to condemn the famous TV evangelist for being watered down and money conscious. But most local preachers can be watered down and just as worried about the bottom line (the budget). God wants His church to return to the foundation of prayer that stimulates men and women to preach the powerful and impacting Word of God.

Now back to the lions. Sometimes I wish the lion would break out of the cage, give a victorious roar, and run up the street wreaking havoc in the city. Maybe it's time for men and women of God to break out of their cages, give victory roars, and go out and wreak havoc in the enemy's camp.

Story 4: Lions—Adventures Waiting to be Conquered

While on patrol one night as a military policeman in Sicily, my partner and I received a report that a carnival truck had overturned. A lion had escaped and ran into the woods next to our base. We were ordered to drive to the area and stand guard. We were to make sure the lion did not cross the road and get into base housing. So imagine two young, red-blooded American boys standing in the middle of the road. On one side we had apartments with thousands of sleeping sailors and their families. On the other side, we had dense dark woods with an African lion running loose. We were ordered to stay on the road, but how could one stand so close to adventure and not partake of it? So we locked and loaded our .45 pistols, and off into the woods we ran, looking for a lion to kill. We searched every bush and scoured every hill. My imagination ran wild. Every snap of a twig or rustle of the wind was surely the killer on the prowl. I began to consider my great fortune. I could hear it now: "The great Sicilian lion killers." High and low we searched until the sound of the radio brought our dreams of notoriety crashing back to reality. "False alarm. The truck didn't actually overturn, and the lion never escaped. Go back to your regular patrol." Back to our normal patrol? Were you kidding me? How do you go back to normal life after that?

How many Christians stand at the door of adventure, afraid to make a choice? Isn't it time to throw off the restraints that hold us back and completely throw ourselves into this thing we call prayer?

Remember, the stories mentioned above are true and are not to be practiced at home. These actions were carried out by trained worldly professionals and would be dangerous to the spiritual person.

CHAPTER 7

TURN YOUR DREAMS INTO REALITY

I ought to pray before seeing anyone.
—Robert Murray McCheyne

A Church Most Pastors Dream About

Envision, if you will, a church that only implements ideas that are birthed and bathed in prayer. Imagine a church where people arrive thirty minutes early to pray at the altar and seek God's presence for the Sunday service. Picture in your mind a local church with a Tuesday night prayer meeting that consistently includes more than forty percent of the Sunday morning attendees. A church that is truly revolutionized and transformed into a house of prayer. You might call it a pipe dream. I called it home.

We lived out this dream and rewrote the story of our church family. Most churches describe who they are by recounting glorious days of the past, but we describe who we were by what God was doing right then in our midst. Remember, history is for textbooks and dead men. The present is to be lived and lived abundantly. The days of dreaming are over. You have the power to turn your dreams into reality.

You are the one person who can grab the reins of your existence and make your life count for something. Let's be clear. If you decide not to pray, then you will live an ordinary and average life, void of any real spiritual power. God is raising up a remnant of people who will change the world through prayer. He is visiting churches that are willing to become so submerged in the presence of God that religion and flakiness are removed, and what is left is the true authority and power of the kingdom. It can be done! Our church lived this dream.

Every Pastor Dreams of What Could Be

Don't settle for merely entertaining the idea of having a church that is active in prayer. Ideas that remain in your mind are no more than whispers of a great day that never comes. If your heart cries out for the authentic culture of God, then you are reading the right book. If you dream of a church that is more than a religious system, then this chapter is for you. Don't sit back in your lazy chair of complacency, eating never-digested Sunday sermons, watching others meet with God. You can meet with Him every day. Don't be satisfied with the status quo in your life. You need to develop a holy jealousy for the things of God and begin to walk out your destiny.

Language experts tell us that it is important to immerse yourself entirely in a particular culture to become fluent in the language of that culture. Therefore, you must totally immerse yourself in the *culture of prayer* in order to fluently speak the language of prayer. You must become a student of prayer by reading books that focus mainly on communication with God. Research the lives of men and women who laid down their lives and gave everything to connect with God.

Short Version of Our Church History

In the physical realm, our church was seventy-one years old. But in the spirit realm, we were only two and half years old, at least from my point of view. I can only tell our story from the time frame that I was the lead pastor, because that was my assignment from God. Here is a brief description of what God did in our church and how we got to that point. I am writing this story because many pastors would love to lead a church like ours but feel that the cost is too high. Many are unwilling to go through the spiritual and physical battle that is required to experience the deep things of God.

Practice makes permanent: There is a soccer statement that says, "Practice makes permanent." That means that merely practicing over and over will not necessarily make you better. In fact, it only guarantees that you will make your bad habits permanent. Practicing correctly is important. Many churches practice the Sunday service the same way every week. Bad habits and all. It will eventually make a permanent bad reputation. I made the following statement during my first sermon at our church: "There is coming a day when this altar will be filled with people worshipping God, and some of you may even get upset that you can no longer see the words on the main screen." Fast-forward two and half years, and our services were marked by crowds of people flocking to the altar to worship God. We set a high bar for pursuing God and sped toward that target every week.

It wasn't easy, and it required us to go through major spiritual battles. This transformation required the departure of many people who were not comfortable with the new feel of the church. These departures, while painful, allowed a new generation to experience God for the first time. We need to understand that it is impossible to move with God and keep everyone happy. A pastor's assignment in life is not to cater to every whim and every complaint. Our life missions are to hear the voice of the Lord, obey His commands, and equip our people to follow God.

Dismounting a dead horse: Learning to dismount a dead horse is another lesson in Church Transformation 101. What is the purpose of pouring money and effort into programs that are no longer efficient or effective? The church seems to be the only institution in America that struggles to get by with outdated equipment, old-school methods, and of course the death-inducing attitude of "we have always done it this way." It is time to wake up from our spiritual slumber and shake off the fear of the future. Businesses that fail to adapt and remain relevant to society usually go out of business. Churches that fail to change will lose the next generation. That weird sound you hear is the last gasp of the dying horse of outdated programs, and that strange smell is the rotting corpse of old-school methods. Remember, the smell of death never attracts life.

Authentic expression requires constant evolution: We have learned to continually adjust the course of our journey because the kingdom of God requires constant change. We are striving to follow the Holy Spirit as He moves and directs.

The church has bought into a secular way of thinking when it comes to church management. We instruct our pastors to become experts at mission statements, business administration, and leadership strategy. Unfortunately, the kingdom of God is not found in or moved by these secular strategies. Leadership principles are valid and can help us achieve our God-given destinies, but we are called first and foremost to be houses of prayer. What does that mean? It means that we place a high premium on the idea that every person can communicate with God. We have become experts in worldly success principles and novices when it comes to the deep things of the Spirit. We need to set aside our desperation to move up the corporate ladders of our denominational structures and learn to bury ourselves in the secret places of prayer. By doing this, we will discover a powerful truth. True success is found in hearing the voice of God and obeying the clear commands of His Spirit.

Our services were described as fun, spiritual, challenging, entertaining, and demanding. But you could never describe them as boring. We developed a strategy for our services that was in line with the DNA of who we were.

Walking the line: The backbone of our church was our weekly prayer night. The backbone of our prayer night was our daily staff prayer meeting. We perfected many prayer strategies in our daily prayer sessions and then introduced them into the weekly prayer night. In the mornings, we marched around our church sanctuary declaring the great things of God. We walked back and forth at the altar as we prayed. Eventually, we nicknamed this strategy "walking the line."

Evolution is a positive word. It just means we develop gradually. We can evolve into something better or something worse. That is up to you and what you focus on. Likewise, worship, preaching, and altar ministry must develop and flow as one. They must align and work together to accomplish what God intends on any given Sunday. Church ministry that does not evolve will not be able to align with other departments. Ministry that is not aligned will not work properly, and people will not be impacted. All departments in the local church must be bathed in prayer and become spiritual expressions of honoring God.

Enough? There is never enough: You need to develop an attitude of *more*. We are never settled or complacent in our relationships with God. We want more of Him, and we are motivated to get all we can. When you feel like you have all you need, then that is all you're ever going to get. These are a few of the many lessons that we have learned as we have journeyed toward freedom in Christ.

Smog-free zone: journey up prayer mountain: Several years ago, I traveled to Phoenix, Arizona, to attend Tommy Barnett's Pastor School. I was excited to see the famous prayer mountain that is located directly behind the church. The next morning, Terry Hull and I woke up early and began our journey up the mountain. My spirit leaped within me when I noticed hundreds of other people climbing the mountain with us. The purpose of this climb was simple: to pray over the city of Phoenix.

As we reached the summit, we turned and began to declare powerful prayers over the local community. The sun was rising over the horizon, and a reddish glow began to surround the two main hills jutting up from the valley below. The headlights of a thousand vehicles streaming into the city center created an amazing light show. Suddenly, I noticed another element of Phoenix that up to this point had been hidden from my sight. But there it was, rising out of the valley like a demonic presence bent on ruining my glorious experience—the tainted air of pollution. It was suffocating the clean air and transforming the reddish glow into a brownish haze. At that moment I realized an important lesson. Physical smog hid the true beauty of the Arizona landscape. I want to live in a smog-free zone, spiritually and physically. I want to live in a city where I can breathe air that is free from pollution, and I want to live a life that is free from the spiritual smog of sin and compromise.

Living a smog-free life:
1. Develop an attitude of expectancy and excitement.
2. Get rid of spiritual hindrances (wrong motives, sin, attitudes, etc.).
3. Cancel your defeatist attitude—"We can do it" must be your new motto.

A church can be many things: a social club, recreation center, or even a tool for politics. Your church can be all these things and more yet miss the destiny that God has created for you. The main ingredient for a successful church is spirituality. The pastor of Brooklyn Tabernacle in New York puts it this way, "You aren't a New Testament Christian if you don't have a prayer life." Every person and every church has an atmosphere. What is yours? Is your atmosphere spiritual or worldly? Notice, I didn't say religious. You can change your environment, but first you must change your concept of Christianity. If you understand Christianity to be a religion, then you can't really alter the atmosphere of your church. We are not part of religion—no, we are citizens of a kingdom. Once we understand this point and realize that the atmosphere of our churches is connected to each member's intimacy with the King, then we can begin to effect change that will last.

Participant or spectator?: You must transition from being a spectator in the church to a participant in the kingdom. Participation in the kingdom is easy and can start today. You don't have to preach like Billy Graham, lead worship like Hillsong Church, or prophesy like Rick Joyner to make an impact in the world. You can get on your knees, touch heaven, and spark a flame that will ignite your community into a wildfire of God's presence.

Spiritual people are fully engaged in the kingdom. Their bodies are involved (they show up), and their minds are focused (they don't check their brains at the door). They are soul-stirring, life-imparting, city-transforming warriors who settle for nothing less than the kingdom of God. No substitute religious activity or man-made manifestation will suffice. They desire the kingdom and the King above all else, and "life as usual" is a death knell to their spirits.

CHAPTER 8

TODAY'S HARD WORK CREATES TOMORROW'S SUCCESS

It is impossible for you to keep your spirit in harmony with the divine nature without much prayer.
—E. M. Bounds

Have you ever felt like God has lost His voice? He just isn't speaking to you anymore. In this chapter, we are going to look at Daniel, the lion of prayer. Daniel was a leader and prophet in the Old Testament. He received a word from God about a future event that was going to be difficult to complete. He knew it would happen. He just didn't know when or how. Have you ever received a word from God that was awesome, but the timing was lousy? It was one of those futuristic, "happening at a later date" kind of words. I have found that the missing ingredient to navigating these situations is patience. Daniel had to combine patience and action to see the fulfillment of this word. He also learned a valuable lesson.

Delay Doesn't Mean Denial

People will receive a word from God and not even lift a finger to work toward the achievement of that word. My friend Daren Lindley once said to me, "You get a word from God to write a book, but you won't even sharpen a pencil to get ready." My grandmother used to say, "I get rid of the little stones in my life, and God gets rid of the big boulders." In other words, I do my part, and God does his. Warning: patience without preparation dashes our destiny on the rocks of indifference.

Daniel 10:3 NKJV: "I ate no pleasant food, nor meat or wine

came into my mouth, nor did I anoint myself at all until three whole weeks were fulfilled." Daniel was learning an important concept in the arena of prayer.

Human Action Always Stimulates a God Reaction

Daniel spent twenty-one days fasting for his destiny. Three weeks is a necessary time frame. It just so happens that I started writing this book during a three-week period of fasting and prayer. Psychologists tell us that twenty-one days is required to form a habit. I like three weeks. It is short enough to be doable and just long enough to require commitment. Long-term patterns are formed between 18 and 254 days, with 66 days being the optimal number to cement a habit. Side note: there are 66 books in the Bible, and the Lord's Prayer has 66 words.

That is why the Bible says to seek God (action), humble yourself (action), pray (action), and repent (action). Individual keys unlock God's blessing, favor, and direction in your life. Remember, God is a covenant-keeping God. He will fulfill His part of the bargain if you fulfill yours. There are no shortcuts and no special deals. God will not favor any particular person, but He will reward and empower those who seek Him. Daniel prayed three times a day and fasted for weeks. What are we willing to do to unlock our destinies?

Daniel 10:5 NKJV: "I lifted my eyes and looked, and behold a certain man clothed in linen, whose waist was girded with gold and uphaz." Looking down signifies defeat and surrender. Lifting up your head signifies hope, victory, and strength. Surrendering to God is important. But you never surrender your destiny to fear. Closed eyes represents fear and hopelessness. The Bible says that Daniel lifted up his eyes and looked. That is why I am a big proponent of praying passionate prayers. They keep you from being emotionally compromised by your situation. Declaring the truth of God out loud forces us to raise our heads, stiffen our backs, and look upward. It transforms us from victim to warrior.

The Quality of Our Actions Is Based on Our Understanding of God

The world teaches us to have a positive outlook. But how can our outlook be positive when the foundation of the world seems to be negative? How could that ever lead me to a positive outlook? That is like trying to find happy feelings while staring at a landfill. The Bible teaches us to center ourselves on the Word of God. With God as your foundation, it is easy to transform into a person with a kingdom mind-set and a positive outlook on life. People always ask, "What is your worldview?" My answer is simple: "I don't want a worldview." A worldview will cause you to be cynical and negative because that is the chief characteristic of this world. You need to develop a kingdom view! Focus on the kingdom and let God transform you. Then you will naturally be optimistic, and your life will begin to impact your community in a positive way. Your prayers should carry an atmosphere of the kingdom, which is, in essence...positive. There are times for deep, sorrowful intercession. But those styles of prayer will not be the norm for our lives. Your prayers should carry an atmosphere that is powerful and optimistic. There is something wrong with a prayer life that is characterized by begging, crying, and groveling before God. God is looking for men and women with a spiritual backbone who will stand up and fight. He is not looking for weak beggars whimpering in the corner.

Daniel 10:7 NKJV: "And I, Daniel, alone saw the vision, for the men who were with me did not see the vision, but a great terror fell upon them so that they fled to hide." You may have to stand alone in prayer to see the Word come to pass. People tend to operate in fear, and many times will never see the word that God is sending them. It reminds me of the following poem:

> All men dream but not equally.
> Those who dream at night
> in the dusty recesses of their minds

awake to the day to find it was all vanity.
But the dreamers of the day are dangerous men,
for they act out their dream
with open eyes to make it possible.
—Author unknown

We are of those who dream in the day. We hear the Word of the Lord, and we begin to imagine how it might come to pass. Through prayer, our imaginations take flight and begin to impact our world. Fear and worry do not enter into our way of thinking. Our thought processes do not include failure or the possibility of losing the battle. We take God at His Word, and we fight for the victory that lies ahead.

Time and Effort Are Required to Trigger a Destiny Response

Daniel 10:12 NKJV: "Do not fear, Daniel, for from the first day that you set your heart to understand and to humble yourself before God, your words were heard; and I have come because of your words!"

An angel appears to Daniel and says something incredible: "God heard your prayer from the moment you humbled yourself and set your heart to understanding it." In other words, God heard his prayer the very moment he paused to think about it. I find that fascinating. I encounter a problem. I stop to consider it. And God immediately activates that machine of prayer in heaven.

Giving the best of your time and effort to God in prayer will trigger a powerful word from the King. Why did God answer Daniel's prayer immediately? Daniel was willing to sacrifice everything to communicate with God. Remember, he lived in a time where the law of the land prohibited people from praying to God. The penalty was death. Yet he set his times of prayer and would not budge, even if it meant death or loss of position. Daniel gave the best he had, and God honored that sacrifice.

You will never receive a word from God or an answer to prayer if you are unwilling to sacrifice time. Time is a valuable resource. In fact, time is an unrenewable resource. When it is gone, it is gone. The greatest gift you can give to God, who has everything, is your precious moments. The average Christian prays three minutes a day, and the average pastor prays four minutes a day. In Isaiah 50:7 NLT, the Bible describes a lifestyle of prayer as "setting your face like stone towards God." The stone represents an unmovable and unshakeable lifestyle of prayer. A way of life that goes well beyond a token minute or two of our precious time. There is a reason that Jesus got up early while it was still dark and traveled up a lonely mountain to pray. Of course, we know it was to find rest and escape the pressure of the crowds, but it was more than that. Remember, Jesus set aside His abilities as God and became a man to show us a better way of living and dying.

He was under the same life pressure that we experience. Yet He understood a long-forgotten principle of prayer. The principle of giving the first fruits of your time to God. Our mental abilities operate at their highest levels in the morning. So we have to ask ourselves this important question: Are we praying when our minds are worn out and tired from the business of our days? Or are we communicating to God when we are mentally, physically, and emotionally fresh?

Your Destiny Cannot Be Stopped, Only Stalled

Daniel 10:13 NIV: "But the prince of the Persian kingdom resisted me twenty-one days. Then Michael, one of the chief princes, came to help me because I was detained there with the king of Persia."

This text describes the spiritual battle that takes place in the context of receiving an answer to our prayers. Daniel prayed, and God answered. The enemy was fighting to stop the reply from manifesting into real life. We sometimes confuse the words *answer* and *manifest*. If your problem is not immediately resolved when you pray, does that mean God did not answer? No. It may mean that God answered, but you have not yet seen the manifestation of the answer. So the next step, as Daniel learned, was to keep praying.

The devil cannot stop your answer to prayer; he can only stall it in traffic. Sometimes that traffic is your worrisome mind or your negative attitude. If you are persistent in praying, you will see the manifestation of your dream. The enemy cannot stop the word of God from coming to you. Yes, he can hinder or delay the answer, but it is biblically impossible for him to deny the word that God has given you. Is your word stuck in traffic? No problem. More than likely, it is waiting for the light to turn green

Here is a little piece of prayer advice. More strategy and passion are required to unlock your delayed prayer. The Bible says that our prayers enable and empower the angelic armies of heaven to mobilize and fight. As long as you are praying, God is fighting for your word.

I know the phrase *spiritual warfare* can sometimes be frightening. It is a term that is often abused and misunderstood. It can also be politically incorrect to use this phrase in the world of comfortable Christianity. But it is your lifeline in getting through the stormy seas of life. Living life without spiritual warfare causes you to be ineffective and useless in the kingdom of God

We tend to avoid spiritual warfare to attract the right kind of people to our churches. But I ask you, what is the right kind of person? Sure, you might have great potlucks and cool light shows, but is that really what the church is all about? Church should be a place where the hurting and lost find Christ and relief from their problems. That can only happen when we understand that prayer is warfare. Our prayers may be quiet, and they may seem simple, but they are warfare nonetheless.

We need to help people avoid the black holes of Christianity. The first hole is religion, which tends to restrict and bind people within a man-made culture. The second hole is the flakiness, which masks the real power of God with a false, manipulated style of

Christianity. Daily prayer will help you avoid these pitfalls. It will allow you to stay aligned with God in a way that is healthy and impacting

CHAPTER 9

A SUCCESSFUL STRATEGY REQUIRES BUILDING BLOCKS

Preaching is not a performance. It is the outflow of a prayer life.

—E. M. Bounds

Jesus took the time to pray every day. He spent considerable amounts of time alone in the wilderness with God. His strategy was to not rush through life. He wanted to get it right, and that meant spending quality time in contemplation. Jesus was not the type to walk the journey of life with little or no prayer. Jesus filled up His spirit with prayer and then went out and poured it into the lives of the people around Him. Everything Jesus did came out of His life of prayer. Learn to be strategic and led by the Spirit. A person who lives a strategic, disciplined prayer life will produce great spiritual results.

Moses met with God alone in the Tent of Meeting, and the Bible says that God spoke to him as to a friend...face to face. Daniel had a habit of praying every day, and nothing kept him from that assigned task. The Bible says that God answered his prayers immediately. David lived a life of solitude and reflection. He ended up becoming king and writing the book of Psalms. What about you? What amazing life changes can you be a part of by simply developing an active prayer life?

Simple Building Blocks of Prayer

The foundation of your prayer life must be strong and unshakeable.

The following building blocks will create a lifelong dedication to the art of praying.

1. A lifestyle of prayer
    a. Luke 18:1 NLT: "One day Jesus told his disciples a story to show that they should always pray and never give up."
2. A lifestyle of passionate prayer
    a. James 5:16 AMP: "The heartfelt and persistent prayer of a righteous man (believer) can accomplish much [when put into action and made effective by God—it is dynamic and can have tremendous power]."
3. A lifestyle of passionate and strategic prayer
    a. Matthew 6: The Lord's Prayer was a strategic guide given by Jesus to help facilitate the prayer lives of the disciples.

What Does the Bible Say about Prayer?

The answer to this question is easy to find and simple to understand, but it may not be what we want to hear. The Greek words used for *intercession* (*enteuxis*) and *prayer* (*proseuche*) describe prayer as this:

- a set meeting time
- a set place
- a set purpose
- an interview

Jesus had a set time and place of prayer (it was His habit and lifestyle): He woke up early every morning to pray on the mountainside.

The mountain has always represented the presence of God. We need to daily make the journey to the mountain (*presence*).

How Did the Original Church Pray?

Let's go back into history and see how the early church members prayed. What were their convictions when it came to disciplined prayer? What would they say if they could look into the future and see our current prayer methods?

The book of Psalms speaks of many different strategies for prayer:

1. Morning prayer
2. Noontime prayer
3. Evening prayer
4. Day and night prayer
5. Seven-times-a-day prayer
6. Three-times-a-day prayer

Early Church:

1. Daily prayer (Acts 1:14; 2:42–47).
2. Established sessions of prayer (Acts 3:1).
3. Lord's Prayer was conducted three times a day.
4. Clement of Rome: "We should do in order everything that the Lord commanded us to do at set times."
5. Third-century Clement of Rome: "God has ordered prayers to be accomplished, and not by chance or disorderly, but at set times and hours."
6. Third-century Clement and Origen refer to praying three times a day.
7. Tertullian, Cyprian, and Hippolytus refer to more times of prayer.
8. By the fourth century, most churches had corporate morning and evening prayer every day.
9. Regular attendance at prayer was expected.
10. Ambrose of Milan wanted all Christians to attend prayer each morning.

The Power of a Contract

God is a covenant-keeping God. He does not reward the casual seeker. He will not unlock the deep mysteries of the kingdom to the person who is unwilling to pray. God still operates His kingdom based on covenant promises. These are special agreements that He has contracted with us. He agrees to fulfill His end of the bargain when we fulfill ours. God has always been clear and straightforward concerning the specifics of this contract. He has not hidden an escape clause in the fine print, nor has He masked His real intentions with double-talk. He means what He says, and He is loyal to His word.

The Contract Is Always Valid

Any person or church that decides to pray and seek God's heart will see revival and awakening. Why? Because God is always true to His word. He says in 2 Chronicles 7:14 that if we pray, He will heal our land and forgive our sins. That is a covenant promise. If we do our part, He will do His. When God says that He will show up when we pray with all our heart, He means it. If you do not pray, God will not show up. He will not answer your prayer if you pray with wrong motives and filter your prayers through tainted issues. The reverse is true also. When you pray correctly, He will show up in your generation.

Listen, God only needs a handful of people to change the world. He has always used the remnant to impact the majority. My point is this: don't allow excuses, justifications, and issues to keep you from experiencing God today. The world is full of what-if, could-have-been, and didn't-know types of people. Kingdom people are better than that. They are do-it-now, pray-hard, and make-no-excuse warriors. God's promises are available to you right now. All you need to do is learn what they are, live them out, and cement them into your life through prayer.

Here are a few contracts with God that you may want to memorize and enforce in your life.

God's Contracts

1. The Revelation Contract: Jeremiah 33:3—if I cry out to God, He agrees to show me great and mighty things.
2. The Revival Contract: Jeremiah 29:13—if I seek God with all my heart, He agrees to reveal His presence to me.
3. The Impact Contract: 2 Chronicles 7:14—if I humble myself and pray and ask for His forgiveness, He agrees to forgive my sins and heal my land.
4. The Burn Contract: Jeremiah 20:9—if I burn with passion for God, He agrees that His Word will burst out of my soul and impact my community.
5. The Money Contract: Malachi 3:9–12—if I give tithes and offerings, God promises to pour out uncontainable blessings.

Great Historical Intercessors (from the book *Power through Prayer*, E. M. Bounds, Merchant Books, 2013)

1. Jacob: wrestled all night to experience God
2. Charles Simeon: prayer from 4:00 a.m.–8:00 a.m.
3. John Fletcher: stained the walls of his room by the breath of his prayers
4. Martin Luther: started each day with three hours of prayer
5. Bishop Ken: praying before the clock struck 3:00 a.m.
6. Bishop Asbury: arose before 4:00 a.m. and prayed and studied for two hours
7. Joseph Alleine: prayed daily from 4:00 a.m.–8:00 a.m.
8. Samuel Rutherford: got up before 3:00 a.m. to pray
9. Robert Murray McCheyne: sleep should not keep us from praying
10. John Welch: eight to ten hours of prayer per day
11. Payson: wore grooves into the floorboards with his knees in prayer
12. David Brainerd: "I love to be alone in my cottage where I can spend time in prayer"

13. William Bramwell: his fiery preaching was kindled by hours in prayer

14. Bishop Andrewes: spent five hours a day in prayer

15. Dr. Judson: seven times a day withdrew to be with God

(Many of these were businessmen and civic leaders. They did not let their busy days keep them from their precious time with God.)

Daily Commitment

- I will maintain a passionate pursuit of God.
- I will develop a daily habit of worship, contemplation, and prayer.
- I will live a lifestyle of purity and holiness.
- I will practice the art of daily journaling.

Resources for You to Read

- *Power through Prayer*, by E. M. Bounds
- *The Purpose of Prayer*, by Myles Munroe
- *Praying Hyde*, by Basil Miller
- *Seasons of Intercession*, by Frank Damazio
- *Growing in Prayer*, by Mike Bickle
- *Prayer*, by Timothy Keller

My Prayer Inspiration

- E. M. Bounds: his writings and practice of daily prayer
- Andrew Murray: his writings on prayer
- Myles Munroe: his teachings on the authority of prayer
- Brooklyn Tabernacle Choir in New York: Tuesday Night Prayer Meeting
- Dr. Yongi Cho: creation of Prayer Mountain
- Mike Bickle and the International House of Prayer
- Dr. Larry Lea: *Could You Not Tarry One Hour?*
- My grandmother, Clara Bonner—a mother of prayer
- My father, Terry D. Bonner—taught me the importance of intimacy with God

Prayer Quotes

- The people God uses are people who are into prayer (E. M. Bounds).[1]
- We need schools of prayer to teach people how to pray (E. M. Bounds).
- Dead men give out dead sermons and dead ministry (E. M. Bounds).
- Prayer is the first thing, second thing and third thing that is necessary to minister (Edward Payson).[2]
- Much time spent with God is the secret of all successful praying (E. M. Bounds).

---

1   The E. M. Bounds's quotations are from his book *Power through Prayer*, Baker Book House, 1972.

2   Asa Cummings. 1830. As quoted in *A Memoir of the Rev. Edward Payson*. New York: American Tract Society.

Prayer Guide 1
Communion with God

You must have an audience with God before you can have access to people.

—E. M. Bounds

Silence is a powerful tool to quiet the noise and frustration of the day. A pause in music is what shapes a song and gives it the power to change our emotions. Silence and quiet times can shape our lives as well. Starting our prayers with solitude allows our bodies to transition from anxiousness to calmness. It makes it possible to slow our heart rates, ease our minds, and prepare our spirits for an authentic relationship with God—a relationship void of the deception of a fast-paced life. The Bible says in Isaiah 40 that God gives power to the tired and worn out. He will give strength to the weak. Those who wait upon God will find new strength. They will run and not grow weary. They will walk and not be faint.

"As the mellow-hearted relinquish control over their own destiny, they become ever more preoccupied with the goodness and mercy of God, eagerly looking to partner with God to bring mercy and justice to others."[3]

In this guide, you will begin with an opening prayer. Then you will move into times of silence, Scripture meditation, contemplation, and journaling. Christians have practiced this process for thousands of years. As you put this guide into practice, it will seem like the world around you is slowing down. The truth is you are the one slowing down.

---

3   McMinn, Lisa Graham. 2006. *The Contented Soul.* Downers Grover, Illinois: InterVasity Press.

I use various prayer guides as tools to assist me in focusing on God. I use this particular guide in the mornings. It fits best with the slower pace of getting up. It also creates a strong foundation for peace as I begin my day.

1. Opening Prayer

This session helps you orient your thought process toward heaven. It is a way of acknowledging God at the start your prayer. One example is saying the following prayer out loud:

    a. Father, thank you for creating everything in and around me.

    b. Jesus, thank you for dying on the cross and providing salvation for me.

    c. Holy Spirit, thank you for guiding, comforting, and empowering me today.

2. Meditation on the Word of God

Section 2 features ten to fifteen minutes of Bible meditation. It is where we engage our minds in the age-old process of renewal by focusing on Scripture. It allows us to center our thoughts on the truths of heaven rather than the circumstances of the day. To understand Scripture, we must spend time considering what it means. You can use any Scripture, but I prefer to start with one of the chapters in Psalms or Proverbs. David wrote the Psalms for worship and prayer, so they are perfect for this guide. The Word is our foundation and our source of life. It gives us life as we read it. In this guide I am defining the word *meditation* as a *tool to study the Scriptures.*

    a. Take ten to fifteen minutes and meditate on a portion of Scripture.

    b. Read a chapter and then focus on one smaller section of the chapter. (Example: Read Psalm 34. Then spend the majority of your time meditating on verse 17 and 18.)

    c. Read those sentences at least ten times, each time trying to find another nugget of truth. Through this process of digging for the truth, you will begin to unmask the Scripture and allow it to truly bring you knowledge of God.

3. Contemplation and Reflection

We will now highlight the practice of contemplation and reflection. In this part, we will allow our minds to wander as we reflect on our day and on the idea of God interacting with us. While meditation focuses solely on the Scripture, contemplation allows us to consider how the Scripture interacts with our lives. How might our lives be different with this Scripture applied to it? The word *contemplation* means to look thoughtfully at something for a long time. *Reflection* means to give serious thought or consideration. In section 2 we studied the Word of God, and now in section 3 we are taking that study and reflecting on it.

    a. As you mentally reflect on the Scripture, it will naturally evolve into a verbal prayer.

    b. Remember, this prayer guide is based on communion with God, so your prayers will be quiet, slow, and thoughtful.

    c. No time limit—this spiritual exercise is geared toward you connecting the Bible truth to your life. So take your time.

4. Quiet Time

In this section, you should have moments of complete silence. It refreshes the mind and spirit. It also quiets the noise of the world that has invaded our senses throughout the day.

    a. Set a timer for ten minutes.

    b. Sit quietly and listen.

    c. Sitting quietly causes our other senses to be heightened. You may notice movement in the tree or hear birds more clearly. I practice this section near a window or on my deck so I can learn to appreciate how God is so clearly seen in nature.

    d. When finished, you can write down highlights of your

experience. But remember, this session is not an experiment. It is a time-tested resource to help you calm down to the natural rhythm that God created for your body.

5. Journaling

A journal is a written record of your thoughts, experiences, and observations. Journaling preserves memories and sharpens your senses. It can be useful for stress management in many different ways. It involves the practice of keeping a written record that explores thoughts and feelings surrounding the events of your life. Journaling has become a valuable tool for recording important life events with my children. I even record their silly statements and everyday events. Years later my kids will read my journals and laugh. It is my way of preserving their childhood. A journal is a place where we give expression to the fountains of our hearts, where we can unreservedly pour out our passions before the Lord.[4]

   a. Spend a moment or two writing in your journal.
   b. How are you feeling? What will your day be like? What is God saying?
   c. Remember, your journal is your journal. That means you should write what you want to write and not what you think people would want to read.

---

4   Donald S. Whitney. Source unknown.

PRAYER GUIDE 2
THE LORD'S PRAYER

Prayer should be the key of the day and the lock of the night.

—George Herbert III

The single greatest prayer guide ever created is the Lord's Prayer. When the followers of Christ asked him to teach them how to pray, he responded by giving them this prayer resource. Early authors down to the sixth century believed that the Lord's Prayer was full of mystery and power, a treasure of immeasurable wealth, and a pearl of great price.[5] I have found this to be entirely accurate. The Lord's Prayer has become my most valuable resource for personal prayer. It is my go to prayer guide and my most trusted friend when it comes to regular daily prayer.

There are eight distinct sections in the original Lord's Prayer. The ninth section, "For yours in the kingdom, and the power and glory forever" was added in the fourth century. I believe that it is a great addition, so I have added it to this guide.

How to Use This Guide

1. Pray the entire Lord's Prayer one verse at a time. This has been the practice of the Catholic tradition for centuries.
2. Pray a segment of the prayer and then sit quietly. This allows God to speak to you and allows your mind to settle on that particular truth.
3. I have provided the Lord's Prayer in its original form for you to pray as a stand-alone guide. I have also provided

---

5   R. Hammerling. Source unknown.

an extended version of the Lord's Prayer with my personal prayer notes (based on the Wendell Smith prayer guide). Feel free to use either one.

Intro to the Lord's Prayer

Matthew 6:5–9 NLT: "When you pray, don't be like the hypocrites who love to pray publicly on street corners and in the synagogues where everyone can see them. I tell you the truth, that is all the reward they will ever get. ⁶ But when you pray, go away by yourself, shut the door behind you, and pray to your Father in private. Then your Father, who sees everything, will reward you. ⁷ When you pray, don't babble on and on as the Gentiles do. They think their prayers are answered merely by repeating their words again and again. ⁸ Don't be like them, for your Father knows exactly what you need even before you ask him! ⁹ Pray like this: Our Father in heaven, may your name be kept holy."

Here it is in the Message version: "And when you come before God, don't turn that into a theatrical production either. All these people making a regular show out of their prayers, hoping for stardom! Do you think God sits in a box seat? ⁶ Here's what I want you to do: Find a quiet, secluded place so you won't be tempted to role-play before God. Just be there as simply and honestly as you can manage. The focus will shift from you to God, and you will begin to sense his grace. ⁷⁻¹³ The world is full of so-called prayer warriors who are prayer-ignorant. They're full of formulas and programs and advice, peddling techniques for getting what you want from God. Don't fall for that nonsense. This is your Father you are dealing with, and he knows better than you what you need. With a God like this loving you, you can pray very simply. Like this:"

Lord's Prayer (nine-minute guide)

Instructions: spend one minute on each section. Example: pray number 1: "Our Father who is in Heaven." And then spend the remainder of the minute praying various aspects of that statement. You can also spend the additional time contemplating on what this phrase means to you. You can also pray all nine section together. This is a shorter version but still very impactful.

Matthew 6:9–13 AMP

1. Our Father who is in heaven.
2. Hallowed be Your name.
3. Your kingdom come.
4. Your will be done.
5. On earth as it is in heaven.
6. Give us this day our daily bread.
7. And forgive us our debts, as we have forgiven our debtors [letting go of both the wrong and the resentment].
8. And do not lead us into temptation, but deliver us from evil.
9. For Yours is the kingdom and the power and the glory forever. Amen.

Lord's Prayer (extended guide)

Matthew 6:9–13 (Pastor Terry Version [NASB version in parentheses])

1. **(My Father in heaven)**
   a. Thank you for being my Father, for caring for me, and guiding me.
   b. Thank you that I can see my life from heaven's perspective and not my own.
   c. "Who has called us with a holy calling, not according to our works but according to His own purpose and grace" (2 Timothy 1:9 NKJV).
   d. "The Lord's mercies and compassions...are new every morning. Great is Your faithfulness" (Lamentations 3:22–23 NKJV).

2. **Reveal who you are (Hallowed be Your name)**

   a. Your name is higher than any other name.

   b. "The name of the LORD is a strong tower; The righteous run to it and are safe" (Proverbs 18:10 NKJV).

   c. Reveal to me the greatness of your name. Help me see the holiness and the power that is resident in who you are.

3. **Set the world right (Your kingdom come)**

   a. Help me to further your kingdom on this earth through my actions and speech.

   b. Help me to desire your kingdom above all others.

   c. I pray for the local, state, and federal governments in America to come into alignment with your kingdom.

   d. I ask for my life to come into alignment with your kingdom and teachings.

4. **Do what is best... (Your will be done on earth as it is in heaven)**

   a. In my life (family, business, friendships): "Seek first the kingdom of God and His righteousness" (Matthew 6:33 NKJV).

   b. In my city: "Seek the peace of the city...and pray to the Lord for it, for in its peace, you will have peace" (Jeremiah 29:7 NKJV).

   c. In my relationships: "God desires all men to be saved" (1 Timothy 2:4 NKJV).

   d. "Commit your actions to the Lord, and your plans will succeed" (Proverbs 16:3 NKJV).

   e. God, I commit this day to you and ask you to establish my thoughts and plans.

5. **Provide for me today (Give us this day our daily bread)**

   a. Give me everything I need today to fulfill my destiny.

b. "It is He who is giving you power to make wealth, that He may confirm His covenant" (Deuteronomy 8:18 NASB).

c. "I cause those who love me to inherit wealth, that I may fill their treasuries" (Proverbs 8:21).

d. Father, remove all financial stress and frustration.

6. **Help me to live a life of forgiveness (Forgive us our debts [sins, offense], as we have forgiven our debtors)**

a. I am letting go of all offense and resentment.

b. I choose to live a life of freedom.

c. I break the chains of unforgiveness in my life.

d. "I always try to maintain a clear conscience before God and all people" (Acts 24:16 NLT).

e. "Love your enemies, bless those who curse you, do good to those who hate you, and pray for those who spitefully use you and persecute you" (Matthew 5:44 NKJV).

7. **Lead me into purity (Do not lead us into temptation)**

a. "Fix your thoughts on what is true, and honorable, and right, and pure, and lovely, and admirable. Think about things that are excellent and worthy of praise" (Philippians 4:8).

b. "Your eyes are too pure to look on evil" (Habakkuk 1:13).

c. Father, help me to overcome temptation and instead focus on my relationship with you.

8. **Protect me today (Deliver us from evil)**

I use God's armor to combat the attacks of the enemy (Ephesians 6:10–18).

a. The belt of truth—I walk in truth in at all times.

b. The body armor of righteousness—my desires are aligned with God's thoughts concerning my life.

   c. The shoes of peace—I live in peace and create peace with my speech and actions.

   d. The shield of faith—I do not accept the accusations of the enemy.

   e. The helmet of salvation—my thoughts are focused on God and His Word.

   f. The sword of the Spirit—I focus on the Word of God, on things that are pure and good.

   g. The coat of passion (Isaiah 59:17)—I am passionate about my relationship with God.

   h. Protect my family as we journey through life today.

   i. "No weapon formed against you shall prosper, and every tongue which rises against you in judgment you shall condemn" (Isaiah 54:17 NKJV).

9. **You are in control of everything (For Yours is the kingdom and the power and the glory forever. Amen)**

   a. God, I acknowledge that you are ultimately in control of all things.

   b. I place my faith in your ability to lead and control my life.

   c. I trust you with every facet of my life and family.

   d. Help me to look past the shortsightedness of my earthly perspective and see the scope of your plans for eternity.

PRAYER GUIDE 3
DECLARATION

*We must begin to believe that God, in the mystery of
prayer, has entrusted us with a force that can move the
Heavenly world, and can bring its power down to earth.*
                                        —Andrew Murray

A declaration is a positive, explicit, or formal statement; it's a
proclamation. Jeremiah 29:11 NKJV says, "For I know the thoughts
that I think toward you, says the Lord, thoughts of peace and not
of evil, to give you a future and a hope." Declaring Scripture is
part of the process of understanding God's thoughts concerning
our lives.

I have provided the following Scriptures for you to say out loud.
Don't rush through them. They are powerful words of rest for your
spirit man. As you declare them, your mind will naturally begin to
align with the truth of God's word.

Align Your Thoughts with God's Word by Declaring These Scriptures

1. "The LORD is my shepherd; I have all that I need. He lets
    me rest in green meadows; He leads me beside peaceful
    streams. He renews my strength. He guides me along right
    paths, bringing honor to His name" (Psalm 23:1–3 NLT).

2. "Instead, I have calmed and quieted myself, like a weaned
    child who no longer cries for its mother's milk. Yes, like a
    weaned child is my soul within me" (Psalm 131:2 NLT).

3. "Meditate within your heart on your bed, and be still"
    (Psalm 4:4 NKJV).

4. "Quiet down before God, be prayerful before Him. Don't bother with those who climb the ladder, who elbow their way to the top" (Psalm 37:7 MSG).

5. "Are you tired? Worn out? Burned out on religion? Come to me. Get away with me and you will recover your life. I will show you how to take a real rest. Walk with me and work with me—watch how I do it. Learn the unforced rhythms of grace. I won't lay anything heavy or ill-fitting on you. Keep company with me and you'll learn to live freely and lightly" (Matthew 11:28–30 MSG).

6. "There is a special rest still waiting for the people of God. For all who have entered into God's rest will find rest from their labors, just as God did after creating the world. Let us do our best to enter that place of rest" (Hebrews 4:9–11 NLT).

7. "Wait on the Lord; be of good courage, and He shall strengthen your heart. Wait, I say, on the Lord!" (Psalm 27:14 NKJV).

8. But all who listen to me will live in peace, untroubled by fear of harm" (Proverbs 1:33 NLT).

9. "Behold, I will allure her, bring her into the wilderness and speak comfort to her" (Hosea 2:14 NKJV).

10. "I said, 'Plant the good seeds of righteousness, and you will harvest a crop of my love. Plow up the hard ground of your hearts, for now is the time to seek the LORD, that He may come and shower righteousness upon you'" (Hosea 10:12 NLT).

11. "No, despite all these things, overwhelming victory is ours through Christ, who loved us" (Romans 8:37 NLT).

12. "The Lord will march forth like a mighty hero; he will come

out like a warrior, full of fury. He will shout his battle cry and crush all his enemies" (Isaiah 42:13 NLT).

13. "Therefore I remind you to stir up the gift of God which is in you through the laying on of my hands" (2 Timothy 1:6 NKJV).

14. "One who breaks open the way will go up before them; they will break through the gate and go out. Their king will pass through before them, the Lord at their head" (Micah 2:13 NIV).

15. "They raised their voices and praised the Lord with these words: 'He is so good! His faithful love endures forever!' At that moment a cloud filled the Temple of the Lord. The priests could not continue their work because the glorious presence of the Lord filled the Temple of God" (2 Chronicles 5:13–14 NLT).

16. "Let us then approach the throne of grace with confidence, so that we may receive mercy and find grace to help us in our time of need" (Hebrews 4:16 NIV).

17. "Around midnight, Paul and Silas were praying and singing hymns to God, and the other prisoners were listening" (Acts 16:25 NLT; hymns were the Word of God actually— see Psalms 113–118 and 136).

Gratefulness Rule

Spend ten minutes a day being grateful for at least three things. One of those items has to be small, like the smile on your daughter's face. Fear and anger sideline most people. It is hard to stay angry and be fearful when you are grateful. Another way to defeat worry is by worshipping. The Bible says the voice of the Lord goes out against our enemy to the beat of our worship. It is critical to freeing our soul from the confines of worry and frustration. Singing is a form of declaration.

PRAYER GUIDE 4

THE ART OF SUSTAINED PRAYER

True prayer requires the best of our time, heart, and strength.

—E. M. Bounds

Revelation 5:8: "And when he had taken it, the four living creatures and the twenty-four elders fell down before the Lamb. Each one had a harp, and they were holding golden bowls full of incense, which are the prayers of God's people."

The Bible says there is a cup in heaven that contains the prayers of God's people. Literally, as people pray, their prayers are captured in a container. This teaches the importance of sustained prayer. You may feel like your daily prayers are insignificant, but they will eventually cause significant upgrades to your character and ideology. It also creates real-world changes in your situation in life. My grandmother taught me this same principle. She said, "Keep praying until something changes in your life." It is the daily habit of prayer that fills the cups of hope in our lives. Those cups will eventually overflow and cause positive God change. Praying is not wasted time. We may not always see the change immediately, but continued prayer will eventually bring about a God response.

Sustained prayer includes both strategic and freestyle praying. Strategic prayer by definition is using a strategy or prayer guide. Freestyle prayer is described as following the leading of the Holy Spirit as you communicate to God. Example: As you ponder your day, ask God to reveal specific topics of prayer. Begin to pray in that direction until you feel released to move on.

Prayer Starters for Freestyle Prayer

1. God, show me what specific areas or particular people you are asking me to pray for.

2. Pray only for that one assignment until you feel released by God to move on.

3. Remember, the key to this section is sustained prayer, so keep praying and continuing to fill the cup of prayer.

Prayer Guide 5
Strength

Every person who does not make prayer a mighty factor is weak and useless for God's work.

—E. M. Bounds

Nehemiah 4:16–17 NIV: "From that day on, half of my men did the work, while the other half were equipped with spears, shields, bows and armor. The officers posted themselves behind all the people of Judah who were building the wall. Those who carried materials did their work with one hand and held a weapon in the other." You must learn to multitask. Live a productive life and keep your mind on your spiritual life at the same time. This guide will help you to strengthen your life through prayer.

In the Bible, an intercessor or person of prayer is represented by the word *watchman*. A watchman has two roles: (1) they guard the city from the attacks of the enemy, and (2) they watch for a messenger bringing news from the King. Likewise, we as Christians are fighting a spiritual battle against the enemy. We are all called to be prayer guardians for our families, relationships, and neighborhoods. Our capacity to pray must be increased in order to watch properly and in order to hear clearly.

Watchman Scripture
Isaiah 62:6–7 NLT: "I have posted watchmen on your walls; they will pray day and night continually. Take no rest, all you who pray to the Lord. Give the LORD no rest until he makes Jerusalem the pride of the earth."

Remember, watchmen had two roles: protection and enforcement. We protect against the inroads of the enemy in our lives, and we enforce the truths of God. We must have eyes to see the enemy's advance and ears to hear the message that God has for me and you today.

Information to Consider before Praying

- What is the overall theme of the enemy's attack in your life, church, and community? What are the specifics?
- What is the overall theme of what God is doing? What are the specifics?

Let's Pray

1. I pray for an increase in discernment of what is going on around me spiritually.
2. I pray for an increase in the effectiveness of what God is doing and a decrease in the attacks of the enemy.

Prayers for Your Church Leaders

1. Establish our church and the vision God has given us.
2. I ask for favor and grace over our church.
3. Give us a long-term strategy for reaching our region and the power to complete it.
4. I pray for my pastors and leaders to be
   a. people of prayer,
   b. people of passion for God,
   c. people of the Word,
   d. people of worship, and
   e. people of character and integrity.
5. Hebrews 13:17 NLT: "Obey your spiritual leaders and do what they say. Their work is to watch over your souls, and they know they are accountable to God. Give them reason to do this joyfully and not with sorrow. That would certainly not be for your benefit."
6. May their sermons to be powerful and useful.
   a. Pray a guard over the Word.
   b. Pray for the Word to have free course through our pastors.
   c. Pray the preached Word to be a two-edged sword.

d. Pray for the sermons to be challenging and stirring.

e. Pray according to the Bible that the Word of God would go forth and not return empty but would accomplish exactly what God has planned for it.

f. 2 Thessalonians 3:1 AMPC: "Do pray for us, that the Word of the Lord may speed on (spread rapidly and run its course) and be glorified (extolled) and triumph, even as [it has done] with you."

7. Pray for your church to impact your community and make known the kingdom of God.

a. Ephesians 3:10–11 AMP: "So now through the church the multifaceted wisdom of God [in all its countless aspects] might now be made known [revealing the mystery] to the [angelic] rulers and authorities in the heavenly places."

b. God, let our church put forth your power.

c. God, open the heavens over our church.

d. I pray for powerful Sunday services.

e. I pray for an explosion of powerful intercession during our prayer sessions.

Prayers of Forgiveness

1. I pray a wall of protection around my life by closing the door of offense.

2. I uproot the deep roots of unforgiveness in my life right now.

3. Ephesians 4:31–32 AMP: "Let all bitterness and wrath and anger and clamor [perpetual animosity, resentment, strife, fault finding] and slander be put away from you, along with every kind of malice [all spitefulness, verbal abuse, malevolence]. Be kind and helpful to one another, tender-hearted [compassionate, understanding], forgiving one another [readily and freely], just as God in Christ also forgave you."

4. Acts 24:16 MSG: "Believe me, I do my level best to keep a clear conscience before God and my neighbors in everything I do."

Uprooting Offense in Your Life

1. I set my will to forgive _____ (*insert name*) completely.
2. I commit to never again speak about this issue or person.
3. Go through the list of people that you need to forgive.
4. God, reveal to me any area of offense in my life that I have forgotten.
5. God, I ask you to remove all remnants and the root system of jealousy, arrogance, pride, insecurity, and the need for revenge from my life.
    1. Matthew 18:35 MSG: "And that's exactly what my Father in heaven is going to do to each one of you who doesn't forgive unconditionally anyone who asks for mercy."

Prayers of Confession

The tradition of asking God forgiveness for specific sins

1. Forgive me, Jesus, for the sin of _____
    a. Say it out loud to God!
    b. Confess as many as you can remember.
2. God, forgive me for sins that separate me from you (both known and unknown).
3. Let forgiveness flow into my heart and spirit.

Prayers of Purity and Holiness

1. 1 Peter 1:16 NLT: "For the Scriptures say, 'You must be holy because I am holy.'"
2. Ephesians 1:4 NKJV: "Just as He chose us in Him before the foundation of the world, that we should be holy and without blame before him in love."
3. I pray that I grow in my character, integrity, and reputation.

Prayers for My Speech

1. I pray for my speech to be holy and pure.
2. I will only speak the pure things of God.
3. God, put a guard over my mouth.
4. Allow me to only speak kingdom words and strategies today.
   a. What you say opens a door to the enemy's kingdom and strategy or to God's kingdom and strategy. Which door will you open?
5. I pray that I will only open the door to the kingdom of God with my words.
6. I pray that my words will be a blessing to people and not a curse.
   a. Psalm 35:28 NIV: "My tongue will speak of your righteousness and of your praises all day long."

Prayers for My Eyes

1. I pray for my eyes to only look at what is good.
2. I refuse to look at what is immoral.
3. I set a guard over my eyes, which are the windows to the soul.
   a. Habakkuk 1:13 NIV: "Your eyes are too pure to look on evil."
   b. Matthew 6:22 NKJV: "The lamp of the body is the eye. If therefore your eye is good, your whole body will be full of light."

Prayers for My Actions

1. I pray for my actions to be in line with kingdom strategies and the purposes of God, for them to be in line with God's will for my life.
2. Put a guard on my actions.
3. Holy Spirit, I pray for you to convict me when I am about to make a wrong decision or action.
   a. Colossians 1:10 NIV: "Live a life worthy of the Lord

and please Him in every way: bearing fruit in every good work, growing in the knowledge of God."

Prayers for My Thoughts

1. I pray for my thoughts to be pure and consistent with the Word of God.
2. I pray a guard over my mind.
3. I take every thought captive.
4. I declare Romans 12:2, the transforming of my mind, to be established.
   a. Romans 12:2 NIV: "Do not conform any longer to the pattern of this world, but be transformed by the renewing of your mind. Then you will be able to test and approve what God's will is—his good, pleasing and perfect will."
   b. Hebrews 4:12 NIV: "For the word of God is alive and active. Sharper than any double-edged sword, it penetrates even to dividing soul and spirit, joints and marrow; it judges the thoughts and attitudes of the heart."

Prayers for Friends

1. I pray that I would be surrounded by godly men and women.
2. Father, give me godly friends.
3. I pray that I receive godly advice from my friends.
   a. Psalm 1:1 AMP: "BLESSED [fortunate, prosperous, and favored by God] is the man who does not walk in the counsel of the wicked [following their advice and example], nor stand in the path of sinners, nor sit [down to rest] in the seat of scoffers (ridiculers)."

Prayers for Destiny and Guidance

1. I pray a wall of protection around my destiny and future.
2. I pray for God's destiny for my life to come to pass.

3. I pray God's destiny for my family to come to pass.

    a. Jeremiah 29:11 NLT: "'For I know the plans I have for you,' says the LORD. 'They are plans for good and not for disaster, to give you a future and a hope.'"

4. I pray your destiny in my ministry and in my pastors' lives.

5. I pray your destiny in my church.

6. I pray your destiny in my city.

    a. Jeremiah 29:7 NKJV: "And seek the peace of the city where I have caused you to be carried away captive, and pray to the LORD for it; for in its peace you will have peace."

7. I pray for the Holy Spirit to guide me in every area of my life!

    a. I pray for an increase in revelation.

    b. I pray for an increase in discernment.

    c. I pray for an increase in prophetic words.

    d. I pray for an increase in dreams and visions.

    e. Joel 2:28–29 NLT: "Then after doing all these things, I will pour out my Spirit upon all people. Your sons and daughters will prophesy. Your old men will dream dreams. Your young men will see visions. In those days, I will pour out my Spirit even on servants, men and women alike."

    f. Psalms 16:7 NLT: "I will bless the LORD who guides me; even at night my heart instructs me."

Prayers for Developing the Fruit of the Spirit

1. I pray for the fruit of the Spirit to be grown in my life.

2. I pray for an increase in my **love** for God and for people.

3. I pray for an increase of **joy** in my life.

4. I pray for an increase of **peace** in all areas of my life.

5. I pray for an increase of **patience** as I walk through life.

6. I pray for an increase of **kindness** and **goodness**.

7. I pray for an increase of **faithfulness**.

8. I pray for an increase of **gentleness** toward people.
9. I pray for an increase of **self-control**.

Prayers for Prosperity

1. I pray a wall of protection around my finances.
2. I pray for an increase in tithes and offerings in our church.
3. I pray for the church budget to increase.
4. Raise up people with the gift of giving.
5. Bring more people into the church who tithe and give.
6. Let there be open heavens over the finances of the church.
7. Reduction of debt in the church and in my life.
8. I pray to break the mind-set of poverty.
   a. I pray for freedom to be blessed.
   b. I bind the spirit of greed.
   c. I pray for contentment as a guard against greed.
9. I pray that money would not steer me away from a right relationship with God.
10. I pray for a release of true biblical prosperity.
11. Bless my job.
    a. Give me favor with my supervisor and coworkers.
    b. I pray for a release of supernatural increase.
12. Declare protection over your finances.
    a. Deuteronomy 8:18 NIV: "But remember the LORD your God, for it is He who gives you the ability to produce wealth, and so confirms His covenant, which he swore to your forefathers, as it is today."
    b. Psalm 1:3 NLT: "They are like trees planted along the riverbank, bearing fruit each season without fail. Their leaves never wither, and in all they do, they prosper."
    c. 3 John 1:2 NLT: "I am praying that all is well with you and that your body is as healthy as I know your soul is."
    d. Malachi 3:8–11 NLT: "'Should people cheat God? Yet you have cheated me! But you ask, 'What do you mean?

When did we ever cheat you?' "You have cheated me of the tithes and offerings due to me. You are under a curse, for your whole nation has been cheating me. Bring all the tithes into the storehouse so there will be enough food in my Temple. If you do," says the LORD Almighty, "I will open the windows of heaven for you. I will pour out a blessing so great you won't have enough room to take it in! Try it! Let me prove it to you! Your crops will be abundant, for I will guard them from insects and disease. Your grapes will not shrivel before they are ripe," says the LORD Almighty."'

Prayers for Healing

1. I pray a wall of protection around my physical and emotional health.
2. I pray for my emotions to be stable and aligned with the Word of God.
3. Stability in my mind—to be settled and founded on the Word.
   a. I pray against depression.
   b. I pray for faith, not fear.
   c. I pray for confidence, not worry.
4. I pray for the healing of my body.
   a. Healing of _____ (be specific).
5. I pray for the healing of my relationships.
   a. Repairing of the breach in my relationships.
6. Declarations for healing.
   a. Isaiah 53:4–5 NLT: "Yet it was our weaknesses He carried; it was our sorrows that weighed Him down. And we thought His troubles were a punishment from God for His own sins! But He was pierced for our rebellion, crushed for our sins. He was beaten so we could be whole. He was whipped so we could be healed!"
   b. Matthew 8:16–17 NLT: "That evening many

demon-possessed people were brought to Jesus. He cast out the evil spirits with a simple command, and he healed all the sick. This fulfilled the word of the Lord through the prophet Isaiah, who said, He took our sicknesses and removed our diseases."

   c. 1 Peter 2:24 NLT: "He personally carried away our sins in His own body on the cross so we can be dead to sin and live for what is right. By Hi wounds you are healed."

Praying Psalm 91

1. I declare a wall of protection and safety by praying, declaring, and living in Psalm 91.

(Psalm 91:1–16 NLT)

Those who live in the shelter of the Most High
   will find rest in the shadow of the Almighty.
2 This I declare about the Lord:
He alone is my refuge, my place of safety;
   he is my God, and I trust him.
3 For he will rescue you from every trap
   and protect you from deadly disease.
4 He will cover you with his feathers.
   He will shelter you with his wings.
   His faithful promises are your armor and protection.
5 Do not be afraid of the terrors of the night,
   nor the arrow that flies in the day.
6 Do not dread the disease that stalks in darkness,
   nor the disaster that strikes at midday.
7 Though a thousand fall at your side,
   though ten thousand are dying around you,
   these evils will not touch you.
8 Just open your eyes,
   and see how the wicked are punished.

9 If you make the Lord your refuge,

   if you make the Most High your shelter,

10 no evil will conquer you;

   no plague will come near your home.

11 For he will order his angels

   to protect you wherever you go.

12 They will hold you up with their hands

   so you won't even hurt your foot on a stone.

13 You will trample upon lions and cobras;

   you will crush fierce lions and serpents under your feet!

14 The Lord says, "I will rescue those who love me.

   I will protect those who trust in my name.

15 When they call on me, I will answer;

   I will be with them in trouble.

   I will rescue and honor them.

16 I will reward them with a long life

   and give them my salvation."

Prayer Guide 6
Warfare

Great praying is the sign and seal of great men and women of God.

—E. M. Bounds

Warfare Scriptures

1. Ezekiel 22:30 NLT: "I looked for someone who might rebuild the wall of righteousness that guards the land. I searched for someone to stand in the gap in the wall so I wouldn't have to destroy the land, but I found no one."

2. 2 Corinthians 10:4–6 AMP: "The weapons of our warfare are not physical [weapons of flesh and blood]. Our weapons are divinely powerful for the destruction of fortresses. *We are* destroying sophisticated arguments and every exalted *and* proud thing that sets itself up against the [true] knowledge of God, and *we are* taking every thought *and* purpose captive to the obedience of Christ, being ready to punish every act of disobedience, when your own obedience [as a church] is complete."

3. 2 Timothy 2:4 AMP: "No soldier in active service gets entangled in the [ordinary business] affairs of civilian life; [he avoids them] so that he may please the one who enlisted him to serve."

Strategies of the Enemy

These are ways the enemy gains a foothold in our lives:

1. Strategy of gossip
   a. Manipulation, gossip, slander, destroying the reputation of people.

b. God's counterattack: I break the attack of gossip by speaking only good over people. I will guard my conversation and refrain from speaking negatively concerning any person.

2. Strategy of weakening leadership
   a. Ministry killer, direct attacks on anyone in leadership or ministry. The overall plan of attack on the ministry of the local church.
   b. God's counterattack: I overcome these tactics in our church and in my life by praying for my leaders. I ask for greater *gifting and anointing* for the leadership in my church. May they exhibit in a greater way the fruit of the Spirit.

3. Strategy of sin
   a. Sin restricts you and constricts you until you die spiritually. Holiness frees you to live for God.
   b. God's counterattack: I break sin in my church and in my life by choosing to live a life of holiness. I commit to making good, wholesome decisions in my life.

4. Strategy of negativity
   a. Critical speech, negativity, looking for mistakes or faults in others. An unhealthy sense of being better, criticism of spiritual things.
   b. God's counterattack: I bind all of these negative attributes of scrutiny in our church and in my life, and I choose to think with an *optimistic mind-set* and speak with *voice of the kingdom* to defeat the attitude of scrutiny.

5. Strategy of confusion
   a. Causes chaos in the church or in your ministry or life. Seeks to bring distraction or division so as to delay or derail God's plan.

b. God's counterattack: I break all confusion and chaos in our church and in my life by choosing daily to follow the will and teaching of Christ. I bind all distraction and division in Jesus's name, and I declare and live with *strategy* and *discipline* to defeat confusion.

6. Strategy of fear

   a. Seeks to destroy faith and boldness. Brings God's people to their knees in worry, rather than to their knees in prayer. Fear paralyzes people, so they are afraid to move out after God. Fear and worry lead to paranoia, which allows the enemy to control our actions and thoughts.

   b. God's counterattack: I overcome all fear in our church and in my life by choosing to act with *boldness* and *confidence*. I pray with *passion* to defeat the feelings of fear and worry.

7. Strategy of friendly fire

   a. Causes God's people to attack each other rather than the enemy. It takes the form of revenge.

   b. God's counterattack: I overcome the tactics of assault that the enemy uses in our church and in my life by choosing to *bless others with my words*.

8. Strategy of defeat and condemnation

   a. The refusal to acknowledge what God is doing and has done.

   b. God's counterattack: I break all condemning statements in our church and in my life. I will *celebrate* the *victories* that God has given me, and I look forward with anticipation to more victories in the future.

9. Strategy of complacency

   a. Settling in and refusing to move ahead with God.

   b. God's counterattack: I bind all tendencies to settle in

and fall asleep spiritually. I choose to have a *pioneering spirit* so I can forge ahead to defeat the spirit of slumber.

10. Strategy of religion
    a. Causes ritualistic hardness and rigidness in our spiritual journey. The hardness caused by religion must be uprooted. Learn to break through all of the religious mind-sets that would keep us from truly following God.
    b. God's counterattack: I break free from all forms of religion and hardness in my church and in my life. I choose to live with happiness and excitement as I walk out my Christian journey.

Declare These Scriptures

a. Matthew 16:19: "And I will give you the keys of the kingdom of heaven, and whatever you bind on earth will be bound in heaven, and whatever you loose on earth will be loosed in heaven."
b. Acts 4:29–30 NLT: "And now, O Lord, hear their threats, and give us, your servants, great boldness in preaching your word. Stretch out your hand with healing power; may miraculous signs and wonders be done through the name of your holy servant Jesus."

Personal Declarations

1. I release the destiny and the assignments of the Holy Spirit in my life, church, business, and home.
2. I release freedom over my life.
3. I release strength into my physical body.
4. I release stability into my emotions.
5. I release boldness into my worries.
6. I release courage into my fear.
7. I release the knowledge of God into my mind.
8. I release revelation from God into my spirit.

Pray Spiritual Protection

1. My family: name each member of your family.
2. My ministry.
3. My church: I pray blessing, grace, and favor over our church. I declare that God's desire for our church will be realized. We will walk completely in God's will for us.
4. My destiny: I pray that I will not be distracted from accomplishing God's destiny for my life.

Pray the Armor of God

Ephesians 6:11 AMP: "Put on the full armor of God [for His precepts are like the splendid armor of a heavily-armed soldier], so that you may be able to [successfully] stand up against all the schemes *and* the strategies *and* the deceits of the devil.

1. Sturdy belt of truth—walk in truth at all times.
2. Body armor of righteousness—guard your heart.
3. Stable shoes of the gospel of peace—be stable in the battle.
4. Shield of faith—stop the fiery arrows of the enemy.
5. Helmet of salvation—take every thought captive; transform my mind.
6. Sword of the spirit—declare the Rhema word of God. *Logos* is the Word of God. *Rhema* is a specific portion of Scripture that comes alive to you.
7. Cloak of passion—(Isaiah 59:17) makes me passionate.
8. Perseverance—keep going; I won't give up.
9. Night-vision goggles—I will see through the darkness.
10. Spear of prayer—I will use this weapon to fight locally, regionally, and nationally.
11. Mouthpiece of boldness—I will speak and pray boldly.

The War

Ephesians 6:12 AMP: "For our struggle is not against flesh and blood [contending only with physical opponents], but against the rulers, against the powers, against the world forces of this [present] darkness, against the spiritual *forces* of wickedness in the heavenly (supernatural) *places.*"

1. The Bible describes the following demonic authorities, their influence, and their assigned attacks:
   a. Principalities—weakest level of demonic attack
   b. Powers—regional power and stronger level of authority
   c. Rulers of this dark age—includes actual human leaders who are used of the enemy
   d. Spiritual forces in high places—highest level of demonic power
2. I pray that communication between the demonic levels is chaotic and confusing and that their connection to humans is noneffective.
3. I pray that the deepest root system of these demonic elements will be uprooted in our community.
4. I pray that communication between the Holy Spirit and God's people is clear and unhindered.
   a. My mind is open to receive from God and is aligned to the thoughts of God.
   b. My spirit and life are led by the Holy Spirit.
   c. Open my ears to hear your voice.
   d. Open my eyes to see how you are moving throughout the earth and throughout my community.

Releasing Angels in Warfare

The Bible says that God gives His angels charge over you. In the original language it says, "God commands His angels to command your life based on the will of God."

1. God release the *warrior angels* to begin to fight on our behalf and according to our prayers.
2. Assign angels to be encamped around certain people and places (for protection and for warfare).
3. God, I pray that you would send in angelic reinforcements

to win the battle in every situation that I name (begin naming locations and people).

4. God release the *messenger angels* to bring the unhindered word of the Lord and answers to our prayers immediately.

5. God release the *ministering angels* to start releasing healing, prosperity, emotional strength, and life to God's people.

Daily Prayer Scripture

Job 22:28 NASB: "You will also decree a thing, and it will be established for you; And light will shine on your ways."

Prayer Guide 7
Spiritual Warfare Scriptures

We need schools of prayer to teach people how to pray.
—E. M. Bounds

Spiritual warfare is an essential element of daily and weekly prayer. Spiritual warfare is literally *taking a stand*. As followers of Christ, it is important that we learn to take a position for truth and at times risk something for the kingdom of God. Resisting the plans of the enemy is valid because the Bible says to "Resist the devil." However, we also must learn to adopt a position *for* something. We must stand for our families, for our cities, and for our churches. We must stand for truth and social justice.

It almost seems sacrilegious to mention the words *prayer* and *weapon* in the same sentence. Jesus used prayer in warfare. Prayer was His vehicle—a weapon wielded to navigate and defeat the enemy. As Martin Luther King said, "In the end, we will remember not the words of our enemies but the silence of our friends."[6] Elie Wiesel, the 1986 Nobel Peace Prize winner, wrote, "I swore never to be silent whenever and wherever human beings endure suffering and humiliation. We must always take sides. Neutrality helps the oppressor, never the victim."[7] We were built to fight. It is against the laws of nature and the kingdom of God to sit by idly as the

---

6   https://www.brainyquote.com/quotes/quotes/m/
martinluth103571.html

7   Wiesel, Elie. 1986. Acceptance Speech. *Nobelprize.org.*
http://www.nobelprize.org/nobel_prizes/peace/laureates/1986/
wiesel-acceptance_en.html. Accessed Jan. 17, 2017.

enemy destroys our families and cities. Prayer is our most potent weapon for spiritual warfare.

Declaring these Scriptures as you pray is one way you can take a stand. I have found great peace and relief from the assault of the enemy when I declare these Scriptures. This process is more about aligning your thoughts with the principles of the kingdom of heaven. It is not about battling demonic forces. It is the process of renewing your thoughts and your mind. As you say these Scriptures out loud, your mind will begin to focus on the truth of heaven rather than the fear of the situation you are currently journeying through. I have included a space between each Scripture. This symbolizes a *selah* (a time to pause and consider). You can also use this time to expand your prayer based on that particular Scripture.

1. James 4:7 NLT: "So humble yourselves before God. Resist the devil, and he will flee from you."
   a. I submit my life to you, God.
   b. My thoughts.
   c. My actions.
   d. My motives.
   e. My influences.
   f. I resist every attempt of the enemy to control or influence my family or myself.
   g. SELAH.

2. 2 Corinthians 10:3–5 NKJV: "For though we walk in the flesh, we do not war according to the flesh. For the weapons of our warfare *are* not carnal but mighty in God for pulling down strongholds, casting down arguments and every high thing that exalts itself against the knowledge of God, bringing every thought into captivity to the obedience of Christ."
   a. Father, we refute every attack of the enemy through thoughts and persuasion. I declare that I do not believe

the lie of the enemy. Instead, I agree with the truth of what the Word of God declares about me. I break every negative stronghold in my life, and I rebuild the ruins of godly strongholds that have been created for my benefit.

b. SELAH.

3. 1 Peter 5:8–9 NLT: "Stay alert! Watch out for your great enemy, the devil. He prowls around like a roaring lion, looking for someone to devour. Stand firm against him, and be strong in your faith. Remember that your family of believers all over the world is going through the same kind of suffering you are."

a. I declare that I am alert and am well able to see the attacks of the enemy. I am in control of this body and mind that God has given me. I stand firm in my faith in Christ, my belief in God the Father, and in His kingdom. I choose to speak only life and words of encouragement. I choose to think only what is godly and beneficial for spiritual growth.

b. SELAH.

4. Isaiah 54:17 NKJV:
"No weapon formed against you shall prosper,
And every tongue *which* rises against you in judgment you shall condemn.
This *is* the heritage of the servants of the LORD, and their righteousness *is* from Me," Says the LORD."

a. I refute every weapon, every plan, and every strategy of the enemy against me. I declare that these demonic plans will not come to fruition but will instead fall to the ground useless. I break off all condemning, shame-filled words or statements that have been spoken to me or about me. You exonerate me and declare me a person of honor, grace, and faith.

b. SELAH.

5. Ephesians 6:11–17 NIV: "Put on the full armor of God, so that you can take your stand against the devil's schemes. For our struggle is not against flesh and blood, but against the rulers, against the authorities, against the powers of this dark world and against the spiritual forces of evil in the heavenly realms. Stand firm then, with the belt of truth buckled around your waist, with the breastplate of righteousness in place, and with your feet fitted with the readiness that comes from the gospel of peace. In addition to all this, take up the shield of faith, with which you can extinguish all the flaming arrows of the evil one. Take the helmet of salvation and the sword of the Spirit, which is the word of God."
   a. SELAH.

6. Romans 8:37 NKJV: "In all these things, we are more than conquerors through Him who loved us."
   a. I am a winner in every area of my life—spiritually, physically, emotionally, educationally, and socially. I am the head and not the tail. God has given me the ability to take ground for the kingdom and to administrate those gains.
   b. SELAH.

7. 1 Corinthians 15:57 NKJV: "But thanks be to God, who gives us the victory through our Lord Jesus Christ."
   a. SELAH.

8. Zechariah 4:6 NKJV: "'Not by might nor by power, but by My Spirit,' says the Lord of hosts."
   a. I ask for the Spirit of God to give me power today to further God's kingdom, to heal the sick, to speak about salvation, to declare prophetic words into those who are confused, and to demolish strongholds of the enemy. It

is your power that gives me strength. I do not operate on my own strength.

b. SELAH.

9. 2 Thessalonians 3:3 NKJV: "But the Lord is faithful, and he will strengthen you and protect you from the evil one."

a. Give me strength today, and protect me from every evil one.

b. SELAH.

10. Luke 10:19 NASB: "Behold, I have given you authority to tread on serpents and scorpions and over all the power of the enemy, and nothing will injure you."

a. Thank you, God, for protecting me. I declare that nothing shall hurt me or my family or my destiny. You have given me authority. I use that power now to counter the attacks of the enemy.

b. SELAH.

11. John 10:10 NASB: "The thief comes only to steal and kill and destroy. I came that they may have life and have it abundantly."

a. I declare a great abundance in my life. I ask for an ability to enjoy the journey and walk in joy and happiness.

b. SELAH.

12. Matthew 18:18–19 NIV: "Truly I tell you, whatever you bind on earth will be bound in heaven, and whatever you loose on earth will be loosed in heaven. Again, truly I tell you that if two of you on earth agree about anything they ask for, it will be done for them by my Father in heaven."

a. I bind the attacks of the enemy, and I loose the strategies of heaven over my life. I loose prosperity in my finances. I loose greater ability in my giftings.

b. SELAH.

13. Deuteronomy 28:7 NKJV: "The Lord will cause your enemies who rise against you to be defeated before your face. They shall come out against you one way and flee before you seven ways."
    a. SELAH.

14. John 16:33 NIV: "I have told you these things so that in me you may have peace. In this world, you will have trouble. But take heart! I have overcome the world."
    a. I pray for a greater level of peace in my mind and heart, for peace in every situation of my life.
    b. SELAH.

15. 1 Corinthians 10:13 NIV: "No temptation has overtaken you except what is common to mankind. And God is faithful; he will not let you be tempted beyond what you can bear. But when you are tempted, he will also provide a way out so that you can endure it."
    a. God give me the strength to say no to the temptations that arise. I am strong enough to not succumb to the allure of the enemy.
    b. SELAH.

16. Romans 12:21 NIV: "Do not be overcome by evil, but overcome evil with good."
    a. SELAH.

17. Revelation 12:11 NASB: "And they overcame him because of the blood of the Lamb and because of the word of their testimony, and they did not love their life even when faced with death."
    a. SELAH.

18. 1 Timothy 6:12 NIV: "Fight the good fight of the faith. Take hold of the eternal life to which you were called when

you made your good confession in the presence of many witnesses."

a. SELAH.

19. Matthew 16:18 NIV: "And I tell you that you are Peter, and on this rock I will build my church, and the gates of Hades will not overcome."

a. SELAH.

20. 1 John 3:8 NIV: "The reason the Son of God appeared was to destroy the devil's work."

a. SELAH.

21. Isaiah 40:31 NKJV: "But they who wait for the Lord shall renew their strength; they shall mount up with wings like eagles; they shall run and not be weary; they shall walk and not faint."

a. SELAH.

22. Joshua 23:10 AMP: "One of your men puts to flight a thousand, for the Lord your God is He who fights for you, just as He promised you."

a. SELAH.

23. Deuteronomy 3:22 NASB: "Do not fear them, for the Lord your God is the one fighting for you."

a. SELAH.

24. Romans 8:31 NASB: "What then shall we say to these things? If God is for us, who is against us?"

a. SELAH.

25. Psalms 44:5 NASB: "Through You, we will push back our adversaries, through Your name we will trample down those who rise up against us."

a. SELAH.

26. Joshua 1:9 NASB: "Have I not commanded you? Be strong and courageous! Do not tremble or be dismayed, for the Lord your God is with you wherever you go."
    a. SELAH.

27. Psalms 18:39 NASB: "For You have girded me with strength for battle; You have subdued under me those who rose up against me."
    a. SELAH.

28. Psalms 91:1–4 NIV: "He who dwells in the shelter of the Most High will rest in the shadow of the Almighty. I will say of the Lord, He is my refuge and my fortress, my God, in whom I trust. Surely he will save you from the fowler's snare and from the deadly pestilence. He will cover you with his feathers, and under his wings, you will find refuge; his faithfulness will be your shield and rampart."
    a. SELAH.

29. 2 Chronicles 20:15 NIV: "This is what the Lord says to you: Do not be afraid or discouraged because of this vast army. For the battle is not yours, but God's."
    a. SELAH.

POETRY AND OTHER WRITINGS

Terry Scott Bonner Poetry

The Mystique of the Tree

Christmas tree with magical, mystical colors and ambiance.
Colors, peace, contemplation.
All emotions conjured by the mystique of the Christmas spirit.
Presents beneath pale in comparison to the mystery of the tree.
For eleven months the tree is a survivor
buffeted by the wind, sun, and storm.
One month of the year the tree is a king,
and the living room is its kingdom.
Adored, loved, and eventually dropped into the street useless.
The end is sad for the lonely tree,
but for one day a year the tree is the center of everything.
Well worth it.

The Audacity of Faith

Faith is the audacity that rejoices in the fact that God cannot
break his own word.
Fear looks on. Faith jumps.
Faith never fails to obtain its object.
If I leave you as I found you, I am not God's channel.
I am not here to entertain you but to get you to the place where
you can laugh at the seemingly impossible.

Falling Snow

How peaceful the falling snow.
Constant and steady.
Tree enduring and lasting, snow topped.

All reminders of God's will.
The key is not to try and control God's will or change it,
but to pray and reveal God's will so we can more easily follow it.
Our greatest frustration is knowing God's will and still worrying
about the future.
What solace and comfort there is in living in His will. Slowly
plodding along through life.

True Maturity

A sign of maturity is not how much judgment and criticism
you can heap on others.
A sign of maturity is how much grace and encouragement
you can instill in others to run the race.

Creation Meditation

The stars, the moon, and constellations are all important to me
nature, especially at night...
The calmness and peace that I sense
when I meditate on God's creation...

Just Beyond the Rising Tide

The sounds of the sea rising and falling with every wave.
White-capped fury subsides into calm, cool refreshing water.
The meditative rhythm of the sea brings me one step closer...
to the season of your presence.
What dreams may come lie just beyond the rising tide?
(Mexico 2016)

The Rhythm of Life

Stars...slowly cascading across the evening sky.
Wind...blowing invisible across the barren landscape of our lives.
Water...cold, fluid, and refreshing.
The ocean...ever leaving and returning in cadence with the pull of
the evening moon.
The rhythm of life and nature combine to create within me a heart
desire for peace, contentment, and serenity.

Words of My Father (Terry Daniel Bonner)

1. May never see one! Doesn't mean they are not there. Angels
    are where we need them most, and when. You'll not always
    hear them, but never stop listening. They are never far
    from us. They are sent of God. If you want to see an angel,
    you must be able to see. They are all around.

2. I know a man...who walked on water. I know a man who
    calmed the raging seas in my life. Yeah, I know a man!

3. One day, God stepped out into space and said, "I'm lonely.
    I'll make me a world. I'll make me a man. Lighthouses are
    marks and signs of the rocks and shoals into our harbors
    of life. Yet at a distance, the light at times does appear
    much like a star on the horizon, and we, like sailors of
    old, are frequently deceived by it. Many times we are run
    aground because of that. Anyway, I have been. If you feel
    the fabric beginning to unravel, ever so slowly pulling the
    quilt apart, stitch by stitch—the quilt you sat and wove
    together painstakingly, over the years—and here, all of a
    sudden, it's beginning to pull apart, thread upon thread,
    and there's not a thing you can do about it but trust in
    God. "Then trust in him" with all within you. I know. I've
    been there, and still digging myself out and still learning
    day after day..."to stand." (The quiet legend...my father.)

4. I wonder if down through the ages if God ever got lonesome
    for the sound of a man who would cry out, "Lord, I love
    you just because—just because I need a friend. Not because
    I need help today, Lord. Not because I'm so lonesome or
    afraid, but I love you; I love you; I love you, Lord, and need
    you to guide my way." Then a new lease on life—Lord, you
    gave me, showed me the sweetness of a smile, you took my
    broken dreams, and healed all my pain. You gave me a new

lease on life. I've never been a man to be stayed by doubts. What I can do, I will do.

5. I feel as if I'm fighting a battle that I'm losing. I'll come out on top in the end, yet it's a battle we all come to sooner or later. The story of, what if? What if I'd have made this choice or that one? What if I'd have done this or that differently? Could it have all came out different? Would things have happened different? I don't know. Would I still be filled with this terrible lonely void I'm consumed with? Probably yes, but maybe not to the extent it is today. Those types of consequences of events, happening the way they happened, very seldom ever leave us completely. I feel like what Mark Twain said in referring to God: "I am a great and sublime fool, but I am His fool."

6. Sitting here…where the river comes down from the mountain country. Gathering up little streams as it goes along, tumbling over rocks, shaded by trees, chilled by snow waters. How it catches the color of the sky and the shadows of the clouds, canyons as quiet as the day the earth was born. There was no vanity here, nor greed, only a kind of quietness that fills and heals the soul. You can't find love—love finds you. You can hide from it though. (Terry Daniel Bonner, Feb. 2015)

7. When you're feeling everything is going wrong, remember. You are a divine project, and so shall God accomplish whatever concerns you. That thing in your life that seems impossible shall be possible. If you're feeling low, God will take you to greater heights. "God is opening your book of remembrance." There is a book of remembrance. You are in his mind. You are not forgotten.

Special Invite from Terry Bonner:

1. Join my Facebook page
   www.facebook.com/terryscottbonner

2. Email me at terrybonnerbooks@gmail.com

About the Author

Terry Bonner is a pastor, author, student of motivation, and soccer enthusiast. Terry and his wife, Jenni, live in Marysville, Washington, with their two children, Shaylie and Trey. He has pastored for over twenty-five years and is currently an executive pastor at Jake's House Church and director of the Prayer School at Destiny International School of Ministry.